# REVOLUTIONIZE
# LEARNING &
# DEVELOPME

# REVOLUTIONIZE LEARNING & DEVELOPMENT

Performance and
Innovation Strategy for
the Information Age

Clark N. Quinn

WILEY

Published by Wiley
One Montgomery Street, Suite 1200, San Francisco, CA 94104-4594
www.wiley.com

Cover image: Ryan Burke/Getty and Shutterstock
Cover design: Wiley

For additional copies or bulk purchases of this book or to learn more about Wiley's
Workplace Learning offerings, please contact us toll free at 1-866-888-5159 or by
email at workplacelearning@wiley.com .

Wiley also publishes its books in a variety of electronic formats and by print-on-
demand. Some material included with standard print versions of this book may not
be included in e-books or in print-on-demand. If the version of this book that you
purchased references media such as a CD or DVD that was not included in your
purchase, you may download this material at http://booksupport.wiley.com. For
more information about Wiley products, visit www.wiley.com.

**Library of Congress Cataloging-in-Publication Data**

Quinn, Clark N.
    Revolutionize learning & development : performance and innovation strategy
for the information age / Clark N. Quinn.
        pages   cm
    Includes bibliographical references and index.
    ISBN 978-1-118-86361-9 (paperback);  ISBN 978-1-118-86402-9 (pdf);
    ISBN 978-1-118-86411-1 (epub)
        1. Organizational learning.   2. Organizational effectiveness.
3. Information technology—Management.   I. Title.   II. Title: Revolutionize
learning and development.
    HD58.82.Q56   2014
    658.3'124—dc23

                                                                2014007576

Printed in the United States of America

*PB Printing*   10 9 8 7 6 5 4 3 2 1

# Contents

*To all those who work to discover
and support the best in human nature.*

# Foreword

Learning & Development is in bad shape. Really bad. So bad that Clark Quinn wants you to sign up to join him in a revolution to overthrow the crap that our once-proud profession has come to.

It's not just that the emperor has no clothes. It's worse. The emperor is so out of step with the times that he must be deposed. Organizations have changed, technology has changed, and the nature of work has changed, but Learning & Development (L&D) has not advanced in the last quarter century.

L&D, which would better be called Performance and Development, is not doing what it can—and what it is doing, it's doing poorly. Other parts of organizations are creating their own solutions. They don't find L&D relevant. They bypass it.

Senior managers say people are their most important asset, but fail to invest in training. The reality is that the return on investment in typical training events is so low that management's attitude makes sense. Training fails to match the way people learn. Training's overwhelming focus on formal learning is criminally stupid. Worst of all, L&D fails to deliver on its intended outcome: helping people get things done.

As Clark says, "It's a racket." Our first step to achieving legitimacy is acknowledging where we are. Change is relentless. Information is exploding. New conditions require perpetual innovation. Time to market is decreasing. Customers are more demanding. Workers must do more with less. It's a puppy-kicking world out there.

In an ever-changing world, learning has become the work. Executing well is not enough to ensure survival. Prosperity requires continuous improvement—and that requires continuous learning.

So what can we do?

*Align learning with what we know about how human brains work*. Humans are good at recognizing patterns and poor at memorizing facts. Most of our learning is subconscious. If we fail to reflect, we don't learn. We are social animals. And we can profit from learning better ways to learn.

*Align learning with modern organizations*. In the industrial era, workers thrived by doing things the "one best way." Today's winners thrive by coming up with better ways. People need to both collaborate and cooperate on many different levels, and that, in turn, requires "working out loud."

*Align learning with the amazing bounty of technology*. Networks put all the world's knowledge at our fingertips. Video and virtual worlds empower us to learn in new ways. Flexible systems support performance with outboard brains. Social networks encourage us to learn and work together. Smart phones with more power than yesterday's mainframes connect us to multiple networks. We have all the tools to create learning ecosystems that support continuous improvement.

I'm not going to spoil your fun by telling you what this looks like—Clark does a fine job of that with case studies and commentary from experts. In a nutshell, L&D must shift from learning to performance. Outcomes are what matter.

Some books leave you with a to-do list of priorities that would take Superman a hundred years to get through if he started last Tuesday.

Clark advises us to design wisely, not to try to "boil the ocean." The "least assistance principle" counsels us to provide as little support as possible to enable individuals to find what they need to know in the world. Let us embrace "slow learning," rather than overwhelm people.

L&D—and now I'll start calling it P&D—can delegate lots of learning to performance support and communities of practice.

Clark provides scores of principles and techniques for moving from events to performance, for integrating learning into work, and for positioning P&D among its strategic functional peers. This is great advice.

I've signed up for the Performance & Development Revolution. When we're storming the barricades, I hope I'll find you by my side.

Jay Cross
CEO, Internet Time Group and Internet Time Alliance
Berkeley, California

# Preface

I am on a mission. At two separate learning industry conference expositions early in 2013, it became clear that, while the technology had changed, the underlying models had not. While the world had advanced, Learning & Development had not moved in any meaningful way. The stuff I had railed against a decade ago was still in place. I was, quite frankly, pissed off. I decided that I simply had to make a stab at trying to address the problem.

In trying to foment change, I have looked at what the research says about attitude change, and one of the first elements is recognizing what you are doing—and why it is wrong. Hence, the first part of the book calls out in some substantial depth just what we are doing—and why it is wrong. I am not temperate in this section, I confess; on the contrary, I may be tarring with too broad a brush. I am not apologetic, believing it is better to be too harsh and raise hackles than to have no impact. Reader beware.

As I go forward, I try to point to things we should be looking at: changes in our understanding of learning, organizations, and technology. While not exhaustive, I do point to a number of elements that have been perceived as important indicators. My choices may be overly selective, but they are the elements I feel we are failing to consider. I also try to characterize what it might look like if we were addressing those elements, both conceptually and with some gratefully received contributions.

From there, my focus is on a path forward. My aim is to synthesize the best information I can find; with pointers to those who are pioneering the important areas. I, from need, am making some strategic recommendations on principle (when I have not found existing guidance), and I try to indicate how I am deriving my recommendations. There is rationale behind them, but in some cases they are speculative, and there is no reason to believe that they will all be right. However, practicing what I preach, there will be a social network that will provide places to refine and improve these recommendations that will be findable via RevolutionizeLnD.com.

At core, this is a deliberate revolution. There are principles behind what I believe and what I ask of you. I hope to make the case, to the point where you are willing to become a signatory on a Learning & Development Revolution Manifesto. If nothing else, I hope it changes your perspective and starts helping you work better on behalf of your organization.

The ultimate goal is to transform Learning & Development from an unexamined cost center to Performance & Development, a core strategic component of organizational success. This can—and should—be done. I believe in the cause, and I have a strong conviction in the proposed method. I am willing to change the latter, but not the former. I call you to action!

# Acknowledgments

As is properly the case, no such endeavor can be accomplished alone. Many people contributed in many ways to make this happen. None of them wear blame for the contents herein; I maintain responsibility as the ultimate curator and creator.

I want to thank Nadine Rothermel from Agilent and the other participants from the ASTD Forum who provided their valuable time and thoughts about the state of the industry. I received very valuable perspectives from their insights.

I owe a huge debt of gratitude to ASTD, including CEO Tony Bingham for approving participation, M.J. Hall of the ASTD Forum for coordinating the Focus Group that provided great insight, Christina Mandzuk of ASTD Research and the rest of the research team for supporting the Focus Group and the survey from which we extracted such great data, and, most of all, Community of Practice Managers Juana Lorens for Learning & Development and Justin Brusino for Learning Technologies, who provided ASTD Research Reports, brokered connections to the rest of the organization, provided feedback consistently, and had my back along the way. Thanks, all!

I have to thank Matt Davis of Wiley as my editor. He suggested the relationship with ASTD that was such a boon, put up with my continual inquiries about Wiley procedure through their reorganization, and served as a personable front end to a large organization. Lisa Shannon at Wiley also was a staunch supporter. Ryan Noll has helped massively in getting my project in on time in a manageable way. Rebecca Taff has been responsible for the copyediting that keeps me on the level, and Dawn Kilgore graciously shepherded the project to make what seemed like an impossible schedule possible.

Several people also spent time or provided resources in assisting me. Laura Overton from Towards Maturity let me have an early look at their latest report, and Donald H. Taylor of the Learning and Performance Institute provided access to their Capability Map. David Holcombe, Heidi Fisk, Bill Brandon, and David Kelly of the eLearning Guild have provided opportunities for me to present my interim thoughts and acquire feedback.

A particular thanks to my colleagues in the Internet Time Alliance—Jay Cross, Jane Hart, Harold Jarche, and Charles Jennings—from and with whom I have learned much of what is in here. The intellectual contributions are immense and valued.

I owe a great thanks to the folks who stepped up and provided content: Allison Rossett and Marc Rosenberg, the latter of whom provided feedback on an early section. Similarly, I greatly appreciate those who shared their personal journeys for the sake of helping the cause: Allison Anderson, Jane Bozarth, Mark Britz, Charles Jennings, and Jos Arets and Vivian Heijnen of Tulser. And, of course, the many people who produced the work I have cited.

Many thanks are owed to my friends and colleagues; many more than can be acknowledged here have contributed in many ways. I have cited those I have found relevant publications for, and you should note those names. Others have provided feedback or connected me to others. They are the colleagues you see at events like Up to All of Us, eLearning Guild, and ASTD conferences, and more. You should strive to get to know them and their work.

On the family side, I owe debts of gratitude to my brother Clif and his family and, most importantly, my direct family: son Declan, daughter Erin, and wife LeAnn for their ongoing support. SCRONsters should be aware that the choice of Drew for the executive was deliberate.

LeAnn in particular is always my best and most trusted advisor, editor, cheerleader, and barrier buster. Her support, red pen to householding, has been instrumental and I'm so deeply grateful (and lucky).

Finally, thanks to you for taking the time to read even this much. I do hope you find this useful, and I welcome your feedback. Here's to making a positive contribution to the organization and, ultimately, the world.

# About the Author

**Clark N. Quinn, Ph.D.**, is an advocate of the potential of technology to facilitate learning and performance. His work has been at the cutting edge in areas such as adaptive, mobile, and content systems. With a particular focus on learning, he has designed and developed innovative solutions for community agencies, schools, industry, and government. The author of *Engaging Learning: Designing e-Learning Simulation Games; Designing mLearning: Tapping into the Mobile Revolution for Organizational Performance*; and *The Mobile Academy: mLearning for Higher Education*, Clark has led the design of award-winning online content, educational computer games, and more.

Currently working through Quinnovation as a principal in the Internet Time Alliance, and a charter member of Change Agents Worldwide, Clark provides strategic analysis of organizational learning and knowledge system design to Fortune 500 companies and government, not-for-profit, and education sectors. Clark previously led research and development as director of Cognitive Systems for Knowledge Universe Interactive Studio and held executive positions at Open Net and Access CMC, two Australian initiatives in Internet-based multimedia and education.

A recognized scholar, Clark has an extensive publication record and invited presentations and keynotes at national and international conferences. He has held academic positions at the University of New South Wales, the University of Pittsburgh's Learning Research and Development Center, and San Diego State University's Center for Research in Mathematics and Science Education. Clark received his doctorate in applied cognitive science from the University of California, San Diego, after working for DesignWare, an early educational game software company. Clark was the first recipient of the eLearning Guild's *Guild Master* award in 2012.

# Introduction

This book was written to answer the question: How does Learning & Development (L&D) move forward?

## WHY

This book is written to pull together a number of disparate strands that have circulated about what L&D should be doing. The evidence is substantial that L&D is out of alignment with what is occurring in other areas. As calls for more openness and empowerment in organizations arise, the opportunities to leverage big data and analytics emerge, and new technology advances increase, L&D is still measuring efficiency, not impact, offering courses instead of assistance in the workflow, and not taking advantage of the power of social media.

This book has been written as a call to action—about the need, the means, and the path forward.

## WHAT

This book has four main sections that tell the story of why and how to change.

The first section shows how the world is changing faster, and the evidence that, by and large, L&D is not doing what it can and should be doing—and what it *is* doing it is doing badly. That's a strong claim, but the evidence is compelling. L&D is largely not taking responsibility for performance support or communities, either for employees or for themselves. And the metrics used by L&D are not the metrics that can evaluate the strategic impact on the organization.

The second section overviews the changes in understanding that have occurred and need to be accounted for. These include understanding of our minds, our organizations, and our technology. Our thinking has changed, our understanding of what makes organizations effective has changed, and our technology has advanced at a phenomenal rate.

The third section paints a picture of what it would look like if L&D were doing the job it could and should do. It starts with a revised focus, includes a self-assessment, and some reflections by leaders.

The fourth section is more practical, breaking down the steps and covering pragmatic issues, as well as looking forward.

## Not

This book is not a final answer. There are answers in many of the component areas, but the integration is new, and a book is a limited endeavor. An emergent community that will be available from RevolutionizeLnD.com will address how the initial ideas presented here can be taken forward. This is a spark, not the whole fire.

This book is also not just about formal learning, nor going all the way to talent management. It is at an intermediary level that covers a strategic element of organizational success.

## HOW

The book starts off with data documenting the state of the industry. In partnership with the American Society for Training and Development, data derived from practitioners paints a picture of an industry that is not practicing what it preaches.

The book surveys a number of relevant principles, citing popular books that document the changes that are occurring in the world and our understanding, indicating new elements that must be accounted for.

A framework is presented to guide thinking about the components that should be under the purview of L&D and to characterize the opportunities, including elements of culture, formal learning, performance focus, social learning, infrastructure, and metrics. That framework is systematically leveraged throughout the book.

A series of scenarios detail what the situation would look like for different stakeholders. A selection of case studies from rising or established stars details some practical attempts at moving in this direction. A rethink that details the new ways in which to address this issue is coupled with the thoughts of two pioneers in the field.

Finally, the elements are pulled together and laid out as steps forward. Considerations and paths to be taken in order to adapt these recommended principles to the workplace are covered.

All along the way, pointers are provided to relevant background information or approaches. Appendices include the Learning and Performance Institute's Capability Map detailing the needed skills, the benchmark framework provided by Towards Maturity's work on organizational progress, and ASTD's own model of competency. Also included is a Manifesto for Change.

## USE

This book is designed to make the whole case: why change is needed, what to consider, how to rethink, and recommended steps forward. If you already are sold on the need, you can skip the first section. If you are aware of the changes that need to be accommodated, you can skip the second section. Anyone who wants to move forward needs to read the final two sections, specifically Chapters 7, 9, and 10. I think most should also want to read Chapter 8.

This is a book to read and refer back to as you develop your own strategy.

# 1

# A Call to Arms

**#FAIL**

Let me be blunt: the current state of the learning & development (L&D) industry is failing. Badly. Overall, L&D is only doing a fraction of what it could and should be doing, and the part that it is doing, it is doing poorly. The L&D industry has, by and large, been in denial and a willing participant in complacency. As a consequence, L&D is on a steady path to extinction. The perception of L&D's value to the organization is largely one of irrelevance. Other parts of the organization are creating solutions for learning and performance problems by creating portals of self-generated resources, such as videos or their own social networks. Yet the potential is there, particularly in this emerging age of change, for L&D to be perhaps the most essential component of a business. This mismatch between potential and current status is, quite simply, disheartening.

Let me explain where I'm coming from. As an undergraduate, I became so excited about the potential for learning and technology that I ended up designing my own major in what then was called "computer-based education." That was a long time ago, but I continued (and continue) to be excited about the ways in which our amazing advances in technology can facilitate learning. As an optimist, I'm always looking for the upside.

So imagine my surprise, ten years ago, stepping away from more disconnected research pursuits to the cut and thrust of the commercial market, to find that the typical approach to organizational learning was not only uninspired, but was flat out wrong. I'd expected the corporate world to have the need and the resources to be doing the best possible. I came in full of excitement to talk about cutting-edge opportunities, but ended up disillusioned to find those discussions were flying over everybody's heads.

A decade and more later, it's no better. Some of the names have changed, the technology is flashier, but there is a decided lack of effort to draw upon an intellectual foundation for decisions. As an indicator, the expo halls at the average learning conference are not only pushing outdated models with little impact, but they're the *same* outdated models. Worse, approaches are being presented as soundly based that are scientifically discredited or have been replaced by updated frameworks.

Consequently, the industry by and large is irrelevant. Let me get back to basics:

- The typical training event returns little for the resources invested. The notion that you can dump a bunch of knowledge into a person's head in a short period of time is a delusion that doesn't match the actual ways in which we learn.

- What we train on is too often focused on the wrong things. By and large, static knowledge isn't going to lead to any meaningful change in behavior.

- How we train doesn't match how we learn. We miss what's known, both in the ways we engage and in the ways we practice.

- How we have learners engage is often trivial as well. We may get them to interact with each other, or the content, but not both together.

- We miss big opportunities to assist the organization that we could and should own. Formal learning is widely acknowledged as only a small component of what leads to success, and yet that is most of what we spend our effort on.

- Finally, we frequently ignore opportunities to leverage technology that are literally in our hands. We don't understand the real opportunities technology offers, are swayed by flavor-of-the-month, possess unrealistic expectations, and, consequently, abandon real value after predictable disappointments.

What is the outcome?

- Folks who dread the words "training" and "learning."

- The use of gimmicks to maintain attention in the classroom.

- eLearning that has people staying away in droves.

- An industry that measures efficiency, but not effectiveness.

Let me be clear: I'm speaking from passion. I'm angry! The waste of resources that results is not only disappointing, it's shameful. People need help, there are people who should be helping, and help is being dissipated in meaningless activities. It's a racket, and I'm calling it out.

Let me also say that I'm overlooking some good instances. There are companies with enlightened cultures, meaningful learning design, effective performance support, vibrant networks, and demonstrable contributions to the organization. Not all of the industry is in need of repair, but way too much is. Most, frankly. What you are doing in your organization is likely to be represented here in at least one way, perhaps more. Don't think you can drop out at this point, because I'll bet that there are situations in which you're not optimized.

More importantly, I'm calling you to task. I want to show you what could be, detail a path to get there, and inspire you to start moving. So what can, and should, the world look like?

## HARNESSING MAGIC

---

"Any truly advanced technology is indistinguishable from magic."

—Arthur C. Clarke

---

If we were doing it right, what we would see is:

- Relevance deeply embedded

- Experiences, not events

- Learning distributed across work, space, and time

- A focus on performance, on "do"

- An elegant segue from novice, through practitioner, to expert

- Social learning as an integral component, not an afterthought

This is not a pipedream; this is doable. Now.

This is not about technology, but technology is the lever, the opening we have needed. Quite simply, we have magic, as Clarke suggests; we can bring anything anywhere we want. Technology capabilities are no longer the barriers; the limits are now between our ears.

If we have magic, the question then becomes, "What are we going to do with it?" Which is a great opportunity to get back to our real motivations. Before we ask "What are we doing," we should be asking ourselves "What *could* we be doing?"

In 2009, SRI delivered a report to the U.S. Department of Education assessing elearning. The results of the report demonstrated (for the first time) that elearning was superior to face-to-face instruction. However, the report suggested "the studies in this meta-analysis do not demonstrate that online learning is superior as a medium"; instead, the likely reason was the chance to rethink the learning process, including elements such as "time spent, curriculum, and pedagogy" (Means, Toyama, Murphy, Bakia, & Jones, 2009). We need to rethink design.

We have the opportunity to reinvent what we're doing. To do that, we have to look very deeply at how learning works, and at what we're trying to achieve. As we do so, we are going to see that many of the things we are doing are not consonant with how we learn and, in fact, are almost in opposition.

To start, we need a core focus. We need to look very closely, with fresh eyes, at what we want to achieve, and then work backward to how we get there.

## PERFORMANCE

I suggest that our core goal is performance, and our role is performance augmentation. We seldom learn for intellectual self-gratification; instead we learn to be able to do new things or do them better. To do things we haven't been able to do before. To do things that will help us achieve our goals. The focus of learning and development is to prepare people, but we need to focus on people *doing*, and work backward to how we prepare them.

This implies, by the way, that it's also about finding ways not to have to put knowledge into people's heads, and to put (or find) the answer "in the world." Sometimes, in fact many times, what we should be doing is trying to avoid putting new knowledge and skills into their heads. It is typically very hard to get people to learn new things, and often it's easier to get answers out of other people's heads or to make answers available in the world.

Which also implies, very clearly, the need to be very explicit about what performance is needed and what is currently being observed. In addition, we need to look at the barriers to the behavior we want. We need to have very clear definitions of what needs to be done, tied to what the organization is trying to achieve.

We should be measuring our ability to impact organizational performance. Our metrics should be key goals of business units, whether it's higher customer satisfaction, increased sales, decreased errors, or faster problem solving.

The good news is that this is doable. Some clear methods are available to meet these goals. There are processes, technologies, and mindsets that together can give a very clear roadmap forward. The opportunity is on the table to move from irrelevancy to strategic value. It is just that these approaches must be the mainstream, not the exception.

The bad news is that, while these approaches are straightforward, it will take effort and resources. We have to get our minds around how we really learn, discover what technology options we have in hand, rethink our processes from the performance focus, and work through the organizational implications. No one said it was easy, just that it is necessary.

## BOTTOM LINE

- What we're doing is not sufficient.
- (And we're not doing well what we are doing.)
- A different focus is needed *now*.
- The elements are known.
- There are paths forward.

Yes, you do have to change. But you can, and when you do, the benefits will be manifest. So let's get started.

# SECTION 1

# STATUS QUO

To have a foundation for moving forward, we need a shared vision of where we stand. We need to characterize how the world is changing, what the current state of the industry is, and the mismatch. In this section, we will review the prevalent approaches, point out why they are not adequate to the world we are now in, and discuss why they do not even achieve what we think they do. It may be painful, but it is important that we be brutally honest.

It is easier to change when you acknowledge that your current state is not working, and there is ample evidence that L&D is not coping well with the changes in the world. How is our world changing? What should companies do in response?

# 2

# Our World

## CHANGE

Our world has changed, fundamentally and irrevocably. The factors are myriad, but as a rough snapshot:

- The rate of change is increasing.

- There is a deluge of information.

- Innovations are coming faster.

- Time to market is decreasing.

These are not speculations. Thomas Frey (2006) cites multiple pieces of evidence for the rate of change, citing deltas in economic growth, astronomy technology, biotechnology, and more. Google CEO Eric Schmidt has been quoted (King, 2011) as saying, "Between the birth of the world and 2003, there were five exabytes of information created. We [now] create five exabytes every two days." Moore's law about the geometric growth of the capability of digital processing has come about with unprecedented innovations in technologies, as well as through refinement of existing technologies. Innovations like crowdsourcing and 3D printers are revolutionizing the product development process and slashing product development times.

We need to see this, feel this, live this! The status quo, doing things the way we have, is not going to cut it.

The consequences of the information technology explosion, in particular, are having a major impact on business. Just at the top level, we are seeing that:

- Customers are better informed.
- Businesses can be disrupted more easily.
- Competitors are *more* competitive.
- Employee skill set needs are more dynamic.
- People are having to do more with less.

Again, the evidence is compelling. In a prescient view of the changes the Internet has wrought on business, Locke, Levine, Searles, and Weinberger (1999) spearheaded the Cluetrain Manifesto. This series of ninety-five theses argued that the game has changed, and no longer can companies dictate the messages that consumers receive about a product. Instead, with the ability to leverage the power of user-generated content, consumers now can engage. Therefore, "markets are conversations" has become the new model. The realization to be gained is that companies need to become more tightly coupled with their stakeholders and customers.

Similarly, Tim O'Reilly (2005) documented the changes the Internet was having on businesses, indicating the characteristics of Web 2.0 and how these characteristics could disrupt existing business. Concepts like disintermediation and the "long tail" have fundamentally rewritten business models. For example, look at what Amazon has done to book publishers and Netflix to traditional television. The web has become the platform for information interchange and, consequently, in this "Information Age," for business.

The competition is becoming more heated as well. Technology innovations are decreasing time-to-market across industries. Planes are no longer tested in wind tunnels, but in software, and manufacturing processes are speeding up. 3D printers are decreasing prototyping time. Cloud development resources are supporting more flexibility in development and deployment.

In 2008, the Society for Human Resource Management and *The Wall Street Journal* conducted a study on skills for the new workplace. Benedict, Esen, Williams, Handsman, Patton, and Rodeawald (2008), in *Critical Skills Needs and Resources for the Changing Workforce: Keeping Skills Competitive*, indicated that the two skills receiving the "much more important now" rating compared to two years before were adaptability/flexibility and critical thinking/problem solving.

The workplace is changing ever faster. A survey done by Jay Cross with *Chief Learning Officer* magazine found that 77 percent of companies said that their employees weren't keeping up with the needs of the business.

As to decreasing resources, while the workforce has been declining, productivity is on the increase. As Torralba (2008) put it in *EconWeekly*: "Increased participation in the labor has grown by less than 0.5 percent in most decades. . . . But output per hour, also known as productivity, has grown routinely at annual rates well over 1 percent, and in some decades 2 percent." In short, people are doing more with less. The layoffs confirm this: Schwartz (2010) reported in *The New York Times* that companies were continuing to lay off employees while seeing higher profits. Layoffs continue apace, with the Bureau of Labor Statistics reporting more than sixteen thousand mass layoff events (more then fifty people at one time) in 2012 after more than nineteen thousand in 2010 and seventeen thousand in 2011 (Bureau of Labor Statistics, 2013).

The bottom line is that "business as usual" is a death knell. How does a company survive?

## CHANGE IN COMPANIES

It used to be that what mattered was optimal execution. When we moved beyond farms to factories, we needed good cogs in our corporate machines. Our business models were premised on replicable processes and scalability, optimizing for systematic quality and efficient processes. We planned, prepared, and then executed.

Now that we have moved to the Information Age, our needs are different. We can no longer plan, prepare, and execute, as by the time we've planned and prepared, the context has changed. We are faced with increasing complexity and ambiguity. Adaptability, not replicability, helps an organization succeed.

With the speed factors already mentioned, optimal execution is only the cost of entry, and the sustainable differentiator is continual innovation. Yet, what works for one is almost the opposite of what works for the other. Flexibility and agility are two terms that characterize the needed response, but neither is an outcome of traditional learning.

In *The Connected Company* (2012), Dave Gray makes a clear case for the changes we need in our companies. He argues that dealing with complexity and empowered consumers means that the necessary stance will be a focus on customer service and on empowering people to make the change. It will require clear communication of the necessary values, as well as a culture where it's safe to experiment and take responsibility. Companies need to be places in which new ideas can emerge and be acted upon.

Continual innovation is really just continual learning. Assuming that employees know how to succeed in a dynamic environment—how to find answers, how to recruit assistance, etc.— is a mistake. The Secretary's Commission on Achieving Necessary Skills (SCANS) released a set of competencies back in 1991 that documented the types of abilities business would need in the future, and they are focused on learning and problem solving. Unfortunately, our schools have moved away from developing those skills (which is separate from requiring them), and it is unwise to assume that individuals come equipped with these skills.

Clearly, different business units have different needs for the balance between execution and innovation, but everyone must have significant innovation capabilities. That suggests a new role for L&D. In addition to being responsible for optimizing execution, we can and should be fostering the elements that contribute to innovation.

**BOTTOM LINE**

- The world is changing faster.

- Optimum execution is merely the cost of entry.

- Continual innovation is the only sustainable differentiator.

- Continual innovation requires continual learning.

There is an obvious need to support both optimal execution and continual innovation. So where are our organizations in achieving these goals?

# 3

# Our Industry

We moved from farms to factories, and our schools went along. While we have subsequently moved to an information economy (or a conceptual one, as Dan Pink suggests in *Drive*) (2011), our schools are still in the industrial model (that's a separate rant), and so, in many ways, is our organizational learning. Our organizational structures need to change, and so do we.

Even in the area of supporting optimal execution, L&D is largely failing. We are not doing everything we need to be doing, and what we are doing we are doing wrong. This isn't an issue of limited resources, but an issue of priorities and focus.

One pernicious problem is that stakeholders, including executives, have been to school and equate school with learning, so they're quite comfortable with training classes. Yet, the traditional school classroom doesn't work either! Mark Warschauer, in his book *Learning in the Cloud* (2011), points out that schools have the wrong curriculum, the wrong pedagogy, and the wrong use of technology. His point is that we need to be focused more on skills than on knowledge, and on application not recitation. The same can be said about organizational learning. We are focusing on the wrong things. We're using outdated pedagogies of knowledge presentation and test instead of problem solving, and we're not using technology in interesting ways. Can we go any more off track?

The goal here is not to point fingers. There are lots of reasons why we are where we are. The goal is to make it abundantly clear that the large majority of what we are doing is wrong, and then to point the way forward. I believe that you have to really "get" that things are not working before you are motivated to change. I want to penetrate the haze that obscures the problems and make it abundantly clear that change has to happen. Then we can address what changes are needed.

## INADEQUATE

First and foremost, we are not doing the things businesses need us to do. ASTD (2012b) reported, when investigating the alignment between the learning function and the organization, that only 43 percent of respondents believe they are highly effective at achieving learning goals, and only 38 percent suggested that their learning organization was highly effective in achieving organizational goals (and this is self-report, suggesting the numbers could be worse). As the report states: "Less than half of organizations have learning functions that excel at accomplishing the very things they exist to do."

Jay Cross and I took a survey with *Chief Learning Officer* magazine that we used in a presentation in 2009. The response was agree/disagree, and a core question was "Our people are growing fast enough to keep up with the needs of business."

Of the 249 respondents, 77 percent disagreed. That is, more than three in four admitted that they weren't keeping up with their core responsibility!

The Corporate Learning Council looked at the rate of improvement in learning over three years from 2009 to 2012 and documented a 4 percent increase. However, managers said that they needed an estimated 20 percent improvement per year. The rate of improvement is not meeting the needed rate of change.

The evidence is converging that the learning function isn't meeting its mandate in myriad ways.

## EVENT-FUL

Our learning model is broken. We're focused on the "event" model, where we have a training event and then we send everyone back to work. Yet, we've known for a long time that an event approach is not likely to work, certainly not for complex skills and long-term retention, from the first basic research on spaced versus massed practice and Ebbinghaus' work on memory (see Thalheimer, 2006b and Figure 3.1).

We are using a method that presents concepts and examples and provides practice, but our practice is insufficient. There are nuances to these elements that are critical that are not making it into the content. Presenting information and testing on it doesn't lead to long-term retention.

Overall, we are course-centric. Our key piece of technology is the learning management system, a misnomer, as it's really a *course* management system. Our tools are mainly for building courses. Yet there are many more needs among the individuals in the organization (see Figure 3.2).

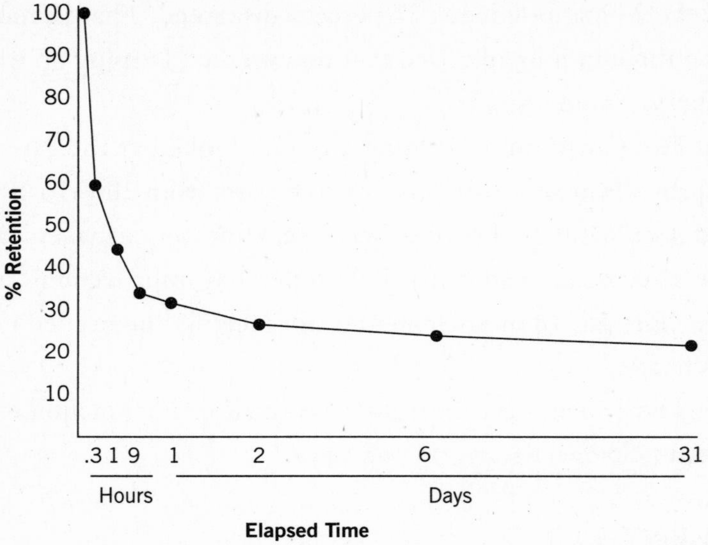

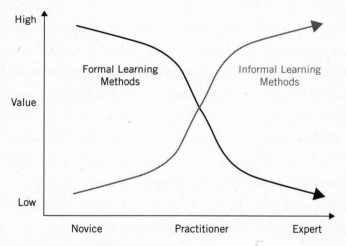

**Figure 3.1**   Ebbinghaus' Forgetting Curve

**Figure 3.2**   Learning Needs by Expertise

We're also only addressing one small portion of the possible audience. Formal learning is for novices, who don't know what they need or why it's important. Once you are engaged in practice, you know what you need, and you don't need the motivational support. You need answers and development: performance support, coaching, and mentoring. Finally, as an expert, you really need collaborators, as well as serving as a coach and/or mentor to others.

As the ASTD Instructional Systems Design research report (2010a) documents, less than 35 percent agree with the statement "My organization's instructional design efforts are effective in achieving organizational learning goals." There are myriad potential reasons, including inadequate resources, but the fact is that we are not coping. The same report documents that classroom instruction is the top tool being used, with more than 95 percent reporting its usage. There is a mismatch here.

## COBBLER'S CHILDREN

We aren't even successful in applying our principles to our own work. The American Society for Training and Development (ASTD; 2010a) indicates that the greatest barrier to success in instructional system design (ISD) initiatives is "lack of internal staff with the required competencies and skills." Isn't L&D the group charged with developing required competencies and skills?

Similarly, in their research on Web 3.0 (2011), ASTD found that less than 15 percent felt that they stayed "on the cutting edge of new learning techniques and technologies." Who else should be on top of these elements? We are badly using the opportunity for digital technology to multiply our impact. There are tools we can and should be using that we are not. As mentioned above, we are not even using the right terminology; it's about managing courses and content. How about creating experiences? While there are authoring systems, most of what we have are so-called "rapid authoring" tools that make it easy to take content in one form—document or presentation—and add a quiz to put it up on the web. That's not learning! In the same way, our use of other resources, performance support or social, is woeful.

The Learning and Performance Institute (LPI), a membership organization around L&D, has developed a comprehensive Capability Map of the needed skills (see Appendix A). The initial report covered the first six months of data (Learning and Performance Institute, 2013). Across 983 individuals self-assessing, the Institute concludes: "Looking at the individual skill level, the four skills with the lowest average ratings are almost a list of the skills needed for successful 21st Century L&D," citing areas of social skills, competencies, and information architecture as culprits.

On the other hand, we can chase new technology, albeit in embarrassing ways. We were swayed for a time by the shiny object of Virtual Worlds, but we misused them, not comprehending the unique value proposition they presented. Similarly, we can get all excited about games, but we mistakenly think that tarted-up quiz shows or badges and scores are somehow the equivalent of a meaningfully immersive experience. We are excited about mobile, so we can put courses on a phone, which isn't mLearning just mobile elearning. The course/event mindset keeps us from achieving real change.

## WRONG FOCUS

If an "event" model of learning doesn't work, we could have a spaced model, but even then we would still be getting it wrong. A present-and-test method is not sufficient. If we want learning to stick, we need richer pedagogies. A problem-based approach is documented to lead to better long-term outcomes (Strobel & van Barneveld, 2009), yet we seldom do anything but "show up and throw up" (also known as "spray and pray"). We are largely focused on knowledge, not on skills. While knowledge may be necessary, most frequently it is in service of some actual decision, not the knowledge itself.

That we're focused on knowledge isn't hard to understand, as that's what we get from our subject matter experts, because they can't tell us what they do. Richard Clark from the University of California's Cognitive Technology Lab tells us that 70 percent of an expert's knowledge is inaccessible (Wallace, 2011). What experts resort to is telling you what they think they do (potentially wrong) or pointing to the explicit knowledge they have. It is challenging to pull the real important information out, and our approaches are largely behavioral, although cognitive approaches have proven more useful (Clark & Estes, 1996). Yet, unless our performance consultants are aware of this and know how to get around it, we're doomed to repeat the same mistakes.

The tools we use don't facilitate meaningful change either. Increasingly, we have so-called rapid elearning tools that take information (such as slide presentations) and add narration and/or quizzes. These tools make it easy to create an information dump, allowing existing resources to serve as the basis for courses. The problem is that this will not lead to any meaningful change, even if the information is available later.

## DISENGAGING

That is, if learners even stay engaged. There is a clear focus on keeping the learners awake. We are presented with catalogs stuffed with gimmicks to toss around the room, we use technology to present information and sometimes to assess understanding, and we select trainers on the basis that they receive high scores from the audience. However, it's largely gratuitous. Whether face-to-face or online, we still see bullet points of information. Are we considering the emotional as well as the cognitive? The evidence would speak to the contrary.

We don't see any attempt to make the material intrinsically interesting and meaningful. Are we truly motivating learners when we tell them the objectives of the learning experience? We can do a better job of helping learners see the relevance to them (and if we can't, we should revisit the need).

Yet, we believe that learners should be paying attention, as if somehow that will make a difference. The attempts to control learning range from "next" buttons that won't appear until the video is finished or some time has elapsed to cameras that stop a course when a learner's attention is away. This is a vain attempt to make up for a failed approach. If you aren't presenting value, trying to keep eyeballs on content is a failed exercise. To paraphrase Dorothy Parker, "You can lead learners to learning, but you can't make them think."

In the same vein, are we addressing anxiety? There's a level of stress that's beneficial to learning, but too much becomes detrimental. We can and should be assessing the learners' concern about learning and addressing it.

Finally, are we working to develop not only learners' ability, but also their confidence? At the end of the learning experience, ideally, our learners are not only capable, but aware that they are, and confident in their ability.

These elements, coming from what cognitive science terms the *conative* aspect of cognition, combine to address a learner's intention to learn. Intention to learn assists learning and lack thereof can hinder it. Yet, the designs I see largely ignore these elements and end up being over-written, dry, and unengaging. Consequently, they are ineffective.

## INSUFFICIENT PRACTICE

One of the key things we frequently do wrong in our formal training is to provide insufficient practice. Quite simply, there's little identified benefit to knowledge dump and then testing after the test; people need to be *doing* to learn to do. And we practice until someone gets it right, instead of practicing until they can't get it wrong. Compare that to professions for which abilities matter: practicing medicine, flying airplanes, the military, or professional sports. Shouldn't we be aspiring to such a level of competence in those we develop?

Moreover, the context should be meaningful practice. We know that engaging practice is more effective and doable (Quinn, 2005). We can, and should, make learning "hard fun," and yet it too seldom is.

The realities of classrooms and training budgets aren't an excuse. Why bother at all if you are not going to sufficiently prepare people? There may be pockets of performance, but the prevalent practice is to not have learners perform.

## ANTISOCIAL

The benefits of social learning are becoming well known both formally and informally (e.g., Quinn, 2009); yet despite the awareness of the power of social learning, formal learning in the workplace largely does not take advantage of social possibilities. The ASTD Web 3.0 report (2011) documented less than 30 percent of respondents using social networks for workplace learning. Blogs, microblogs, and other such tools were used even less frequently.

Formally, learners benefit from interacting with one another. Their interactions create opportunities to reactivate and strengthen understanding, particularly through learning the ways in which others interpret a situation. Yet, even in traditional classrooms, we don't see social activities used systematically to facilitate learning.

Informally, the power of interaction is increasingly recognized as the core mechanism to meet the demands for more agility in organizations. Both in development of individuals, and in creating new solutions, productive communication and collaboration are seen as critical. Yet, neither is the focus of the typical L&D organization.

There are concerns about quality and messaging. I recognize that there are compliance issues where, for instance, personnel at medical firms have to be scrupulous in what they can say. But these are solved problems. If these people have phones and email; they have social media. Yes, there are new social media, but somehow these are perceived as "different." I don't get it.

## UNRESOLVED

Beyond formal learning, we are also not meeting our needs by using performance support. Less than 20 percent report that they can find what they need on the first try (ASTD, 2011).

We are also not using performance support as a solution. Whether designing solutions or leveraging those created by others, we are missing the opportunity to meet needs in more efficient ways.

Many times, people don't need courses; they'd be fine with just the facts, just the information. But the industry seems incapable of making job aids. Beyond novices, practitioners don't typically need the full wrapping of courses; they can learn from just the information. They know what they need and why it's important. And yet we still produce courses.

Worse, when we do provide resources, we tend to provide them in ways that represent where they came from, not how people think about them. We see resources aggregated by business unit, not by how people need to find and use them. We have both insufficient design and ineffective information architecture behind it. Good usability suggests designing for the need, but that focus is too often missing when providing support.

## RIGID

Overall, we are not tapping into informal learning in any meaningful way. We know that informal learning is responsible for roughly 80 percent of workplace learning (a result robustly revealed in many studies). The industry recognizes this. ASTD's (2013) study on informal learning reports that 97 percent of respondents indicated informal learning played some role in their organizational learning. On the other hand, more than 75 percent had no informal learning programs in place.

While supporting informal learning may seem like an oxymoron, some very specific and useful activities can facilitate informal learning outcomes. For example, in *70:20:10 Framework Explained* (2013), Charles Jennings reports on Corporate Leadership Council results showing that workers with managers effective at developing teams outperform those without such managers by 25 percent.

## MISMEASURED

What we measure is also misapplied. If salespeople reported on cost per phone call and number of miles per day, instead of on success rates in closing deals, you should properly fire them. Yet, we are measuring the equivalent. We are worried about the efficiency and not about whether there is any effectiveness. In the ASTD State of the Industry Report (2012a), the very first section (titled "Efficiencies and Expenditures") is about time or costs, but it's not tied to impact on the business. As Gloria Gery famously said: "We might as well weigh them!"

The closest anyone comes to meaningful measurement is assessing L&D expenditure as a percentage of revenue or profit. While this does assess the value, this metric would seek to drive L&D expenditures to a minimum instead of assessing the unique contribution that L&D makes to organizational success. ASTD does provide benchmarks, comparing average results to award-winning companies and to the largest companies, but the overall relationship to impact is indirect.

## MYTHED FOUNDATIONS

We also labor under a couple of prevalent, yet mistaken myths that we can't seem to shake. Mantras like "learning styles" and "generational differences" continue to pop up like gophers, despite robust efforts to stamp them out. In case you've not yet been exposed to the problems with these concepts, let me elaborate.

When discussing *learning styles*, the prevalent belief is that we should adapt to learners. The premise is appealing, since it's patently obvious that learners are different from one another. Yet, the research says otherwise: a commissioned meta-analysis for the American Psychological Science Society revealed that there was no evidence that adapting to the learner's style was of any use (Pashler, McDaniel, Rohrer, & Bjork, 2008). Their advice is to use the best learning design, period.

Well, certainly we might still want to characterize learners for their own benefit. The problem is that there's no psychometrically valid instrument to do it! A commissioned study in the UK reviewed a number of different representative instruments and found that no major instrument met the test of necessary rigor (Coffield, Moseley, Hall, & Ecclestone, 2004). Yes, learners differ, but in ways that are not consistent across context.

The other myth is that *learners differ by generation*. The claim is that Baby Boomers are fundamentally different from Millennials, and other pairings, in important ways. However, this doesn't stand up to scrutiny either. Blauth, McDaniel, Perrin, and Perrin (2011), in a broad survey, conclude that "today's popular view of the generations has little basis in science."

A related myth is the one about "digital natives." Supposedly, the fact that the new workforce has grown up in a digitally enabled world means they have technology skills "baked in." However, this is not the case. For instance, Helsper and Enyon (2009) conclude that the evidence "does not support the view that there are unbridgeable differences between those who can be classified as digital natives or digital immigrants based on when they are born."

The list of myths continues. Will Thalheimer has demonstrated that the myths surrounding Dale's Cone and the percentages of how much you remember by a variety of learning methods (2006a) are bogus. Our field will lack credibility as long as we continue to allow unsubstantiated models to persist and propagate.

## BARRIERS

There are barriers to change, certainly. They range from stakeholders and vendors to our processes and models.

Our stakeholders are not necessarily interested in knowing the details of our pedagogies, and most of them had the typical school experience and are comfortable with that model. It takes effort for them to consider alternatives, and they are comfortable now. It is clear that many are having business success regardless, and feel comfortable that they are in line with what everybody else is doing. They are not (yet) examining the underlying value. However, that does not make it right.

Our vendors also, understandably, have a vested interest in the status quo and progress within their constraints. Pragmatically, they have aligned to the way things are being done, and likely have been burned when investing in new directions. While a number of new names show up regularly, the products have not really changed: we have LMSs and rapid elearning tools, and have had for more than a decade. We also have training solutions, train-the-trainer opportunities, and outsourcing of design and development. And why should they change?

Our models support courses. The ADDIE process (Analysis, Design, Development, Implementation, and Evaluation) that is the epitome of the industry is characterized by courses. While it can apply more broadly, the typical interpretation is to develop courses. Similarly, while Kirkpatrick's metrics model isn't specific to formal learning, that's how the materials are presented.

## NO CREDIBILITY

The consequences of this are robust. The first element to be cut when budgets are tight is the learning unit. The learning unit typically is not at the executive table. The relevance of learning to the organization isn't clear to the practitioners, let alone to the decision-makers. And yet, particularly going forward, learning & development is going to be critical. This misalignment is as staggering as it is perplexing.

The point is, the world's changing faster, and L&D isn't similarly adapting. Yet we must!

## BOTTOM LINE

We are far from doing what we should, and what we are doing we are not doing well:

- Formal learning cannot be just about knowledge dump and knowledge test.

- Formal learning cannot meet all organizational learning needs.

*(Continued)*

- Performance support and social learning provide needed options.

- Performance support and social learning can be supported.

- We can do better.

The path to doing better is to get our minds around what we now know about learning, about working together, and about the tools we have in hand, and then align our approaches and processes to the future, not the past.

# SECTION 2

# "TO HAND"

**W**hile much of what we know about how we learn is not new, it really has not penetrated into L&D yet. There is new information about how we work and play together, and our technology has advanced, too. These are the elements we have "to hand," and we need to deeply understand them if we are to put them together into a coherent picture of the future.

# 4

# Our Brains

Our picture of the brain as a logic machine, processing rationally, has been broken. The evidence is overwhelming that thinking is effortful, and we work very hard to put our solutions out in the world rather than keep them in our heads. As Andy Clark (1996) says in *Being There*, we must "abandon the idea of an executive center where the brain carries out high-level reasoning." We build tools, reminders, notes, and other ways to avoid having to think.

At core, our brains are really good at pattern-matching and meaning-making. On the other hand, we are really bad at remembering rote information and executing tasks repeatedly without errors. We have limited working memory and trouble focusing our attention appropriately. Moreover, we only process a small part of reality. Also, we interact with others; in fact, some argue that all learning is inherently social. As a consequence, we have developed rich tools to scaffold our cognitive tasks.

Our species has in many ways survived because we learned how to physically augment our resources: we created shelter, ways to store water and secure food consistently, and even to control fire to heat and cook. We've gone beyond, to thrive, by augmenting our brains. We have created books to remember things perfectly when we can't. We have developed external representations like the abacus to support our limited working memory on complex calculations. We use cameras and audio recorders to capture what actually occurs. And we have developed rich tools to communicate language, images, and more over distances to support our communication.

Atul Gawande (2010), in *The Checklist Manifesto*, details how small tools like checklists provided support to vastly improve outcomes in medical care, despite the expertise of the doctors and nurses. Being human, small but crucial details escaped them. Once checklists were trialed and refined, huge gains were seen in patient survivability. This isn't limited to the developing world. In fields like flight and construction, where errors can cost lives, rich tools are used to support not making mistakes, communicating, and more.

Our mental architecture is both awesome in capability and fundamentally limited. That is why Douglas Engelbart focused on a system called Augment, looking at how we could use technology to supplement our brains (Landau & Clegg, 2009). When we are augmented with capabilities provided by technologies that handle well what we do not, and vice versa, in ways consonant with how we think, the opportunities are huge.

## OUR BRAINS IN ACTION

To support our performance, we have to go beyond how we understand the world and look at how we interact in order to change the world. How do we make decisions? How do we solve problems? The answers are there, but they are not what we thought.

Much of what we do, we do in an action loop on our well-practiced mechanisms, only bringing in conscious deliberation when we face a problem we do not have a solution for. We have worked hard to put all the things we know we have to do but do not want to spend effort on in that loop: the ability to walk, speak a language, or do certain calculations. When we are faced with unpracticed situations, we break out of our loops.

Daniel Kahneman, in *Thinking Fast and Slow* (2011), paints a picture of two systems of thinking, the first of which is the quick "known" answer. The second way of thinking is effortful and quickly degrades, yet that is the way we are supposed to solve new problems. However, we often find that people use the first system that chooses an emergent answer and use the second system to justify the choice. The problem, of course, is that the first system shouldn't be trusted in areas outside developed expertise.

When we do not have the answer at hand, we need to take a different approach. In previous work (e.g., Quinn, 2011), I've made the case that the way we work in the world is through action and breakdown (see Figure 4.1). We act when we can, doing our work in a relatively straightforward (even auto-mated) way, but occasionally we run into a situation that is not in our repertoire (e.g., a problematic customer or situation). Then we go into more deliberate conscious work.

When we break out of our routine and are faced with a new problem, we prefer to have an answer available. Here is where we ask other people or look for a resource. If we do have to problem solve, if we can't find the answer, we need different

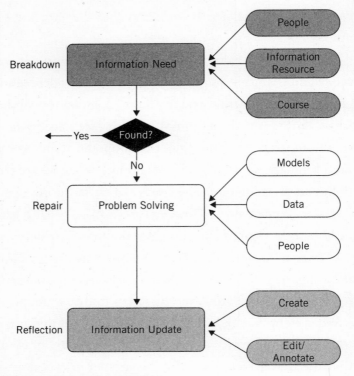

**Figure 4.1** Acting in the World

support. We may need resources such as data to analyze to look for patterns or models to apply that might fit the situation and provide guidance. And we might need people with necessary or complementary skills. If we find the answer, we should update the information in the world, so no one else has to solve the same problem.

It is also increasingly recognized that reflection is a critical part of the loop. When we solve a problem, we can go back into action without thinking about the solution, but we could be thinking how we might not have to solve that same problem again, how we might solve similar problems in the future, and even what we might do to change our action loop to minimize or avoid those problems in the future. In cognitive science, this is called meta-cognition, or thinking about thinking. The most effective thinkers do spend time reflecting and actively improving their own thinking.

We also need to be clear that all our thinking isn't in our heads. We distribute cognition across our tools and among others (Hutchins, 1996). This means that we *should* not, as well as cannot, attempt to put all information in our heads. Putting information into the world and designing rich support structures is very much a part of creating effective solutions to organizational needs. To counter those gaps in our thinking and our limited processing capability (as Kahneman also points out, that second system of effortful thinking fatigues quickly), we should focus on minimizing the cognitive load we place on people performing critical tasks.

The notion that the proper approach to work is focused attention on the task for extended periods isn't viable anymore either. Cathy Davidson, in her book *Now You See It* (2012), shows that we are much less focused than we think, and that focusing has tradeoffs versus noticing discrepancies that could be opportunities. Really, we need to be doing challenging work that interests us, as Dan Pink (2011) tells us, and we have to work less to try to enforce people's attention to the task.

## OUR BRAINS ON LEARNING

We need to recognize that the development of learners from novices to experts isn't a continual slope and that learners need different support at different times. Initially, as a novice, learners don't know what they need to know, nor why it's important.

Once they're doing the task, they start knowing what they need and why and are looking for resources, such as small bits of information or "how to" tools such as videos, checklists, and the like, to do the job, as well as coaching and mentoring to develop their skills.

The fact is that our learning isn't likely to come by chance, certainly not efficiently, nor from information. One must *do* to learn to do. The compilation of knowledge to action occurs through repeated application of concept to context, that is, practice.

Learning is a process of practice and reflection, and instruction is designed practice and guided reflection. This doesn't, and fundamentally cannot, come from knowledge dump and knowledge test. In cognitive science, we call this "inert knowledge." You'll pass a test on it, but when it's relevant in the workplace, it won't even be activated!

We need to look at the details of what research informs us about meaningful practice, creating an evidence-based learning. Various compilations have emerged. Bransford, Brown, and Cocking (2000) summarized *How People Learn*, and subsequently Koedinger, Corbett, and Perfetti (2012) summarized the latest cognitive research for instruction. While research is ongoing, a rich picture of the elements that lead to successful learning emerges.

What's needed is deep and meaningful practice. Research on experts shows that, as we continue to develop, our ability moves from explicit to tacit, effectively being compiled below our conscious accessibility. To create expertise, we need practice. Practice has to be meaningful, tightly coupled, and with sufficient quantity to develop not just capability, but also confidence. Let's unpack these elements.

In 2005, I wrote *Engaging Learning* (Quinn, 2005), a book on how to design deep and meaningful practice. In it, I made the case for practice, in either real or fantastic settings, that embedded the decisions learners had to be able to make. The underlying principle was a perfect alignment between the elements that make effective practice and the elements that lead to an engaging experience. In fact, it is really about creating simulation games that provide deep practice: contextualized and variable performance with adaptability and replayability. I included the steps to reliably design such practice, as otherwise it's an unfulfilled promise and not a viable proposition.

Our learning has to be challenging. There's what Vygotsky (1978) termed the Zone of Proximal Development, which captures the concept of learning in a space of practice beyond your current capability, but not so far beyond your ability that you can't succeed. Too easy and learners are bored; too hard and they're frustrated. Striking this balance leads to optimal learning. The end result is the ability to make the claim "learning can, and should, be hard fun."

Practice also needs to be spaced (see Figure 4.2). As should be clear, sufficient practice to compile knowledge that is available "on tap" suggests considerable practice. However, it's also the case that this practice generally cannot occur from a single event. The way learning works is by strengthening associations, and there is only so much association strengthening that can happen in the brain in one day before sleep is needed to replenish the system. A steady dose of practice over a sustained period is the prescription.

We also need to recognize that learning is not a purely cognitive exercise. Cognitive science breaks thinking up into three components: the cognitive we are familiar with; affective, or who we are in terms of our psychological makeup; and

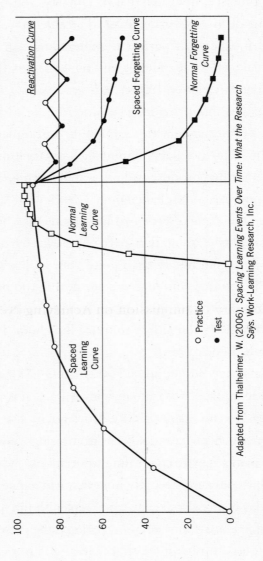

Adapted from Thalheimer, W. (2006). *Spacing Learning Events Over Time: What the Research Says.* Work-Learning Research, Inc.

**Figure 4.2** Spaced Learning

"conative," or our intention to learn. At least two factors have an influence here, motivation to learn and anxiety about the learning experience. The former facilitates learning, and the latter can interfere. A small amount of anxiety may actually facilitate learning, but too much can hinder outcomes.

Finally, we should recognize that, just as meta-cognition is valuable, so too is meta-learning, or learning to learn (Cross & Quinn, 2002). Individuals can be more or less efficient at learning. A number of meta-learning elements play a role. The learners' epistemological stance (beliefs about learning) can affect the mesh between their approach and the intended approach. Similarly, learners can have beliefs about what processes facilitate or interfere with learning. Self-learning skills should not be assumed and can be developed. It may well be that the best investment to make in learning is facilitating self-learning skills! For example, the competencies associated with the Secretary's Commission on Achieving Necessary Skills (SCANS; 1991) provide a rich suite of abilities to succeed, including how to critically think, research, communicate, and more.

Overall, we need to shift our focus from a learning event to a focus on a learning experience. We need to shift to thinking about what learners do, in context, their emotional states, the resources available to them, and the trajectory they take from initiate to performer. As one way to reshape thinking, I have discussed an activity-based learning model (see Figure 4.3), one that considers a curriculum to be not a collection of knowledge but instead a series of activities.

The perspective here is to think of activities the learner performs that build skills, with content available as resources to

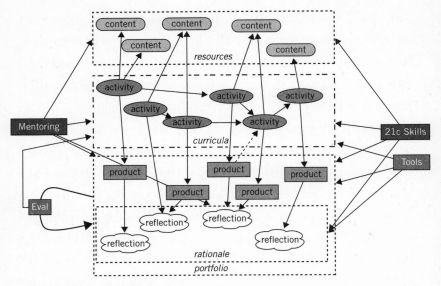

**Figure 4.3** Activity-Centered Curriculum

support that performance. The activities can be individual or group, and embedded, with one activity feeding into another (e.g., a design project that has an initial description to be reviewed, followed by actually developing the proposed design). The outputs of the performances are tangible, whether documents, performances, or objects. Associated with these outcomes are rationales, describing the thinking that led to the product. This structure naturally embeds 21st Century skills and the use of tools. A learner's actions and artifacts provide the basis for evaluation and mentoring.

The products and rationales provide a basis for feedback, whether from fellow participants or from a facilitator (typically, an instructor). Ultimately, the choices of tasks and products become the learner's responsibility, scaffolding them to a self-learning capability.

Note that this is when we really do need to learn, but what you should have inferred from the above section on how we perform is that learning isn't the only path to performance. We can often use resources instead of learning by putting the information "in the world." Given that we are not good at remembering rote information, we should not try to cram it into people's heads (except in rare instances when performers both need the information "to hand" and there are no resources to provide (such as when pilots' hands, eyes, and ears are busy in an emergency).

Moreover, if the performers are going to be using resources in the performance experience, they should be using the same resources in the learning experience.

## BOTTOM LINE

Together, this picture of how our brains work suggests a number of considerations for supporting organizational performance:

- Conscious work is valuable but challenging.

- Most of our work is done subconsciously.

- Errors can arise from our subconscious system working outside of its realm of competence.

- Errors also can arise from our conscious problem solving being overtaxed.

- Optimal execution requires great resources and deep practice.

- Formal learning is expensive.

We now move on to look at how we work together and achieve continual innovation.

# 5

# Our Organizations

The old way of working was to plan, prepare, and execute. We had the luxury of time. We could decide what course of action to take and what the outcomes could be, and then train folks to execute against it. Front-line workers were, largely, machines. The time-space-motion measurements that defined Taylorism (Taylor, 1911), looking for optimal mechanical performance, were the order of the day. Our training was for an Industrial Age, and optimal execution was key.

That world is gone. We now live in an era of continual change, with more ambiguous problems, shifting contexts, and unique situations. The ability to be more agile while maintaining resiliency is a necessity, and continual innovation is required. Organizations need to tap into the success secrets of extremophiles, organisms that thrive in hostile climates (Clegg & Quinn, 2004). What do we need?

The goal is to achieve continual innovation. We need the ability both to solve a unique immediate problem and to develop new products and services, more closely aligning

47

ourselves with the market and our customers. This comes from two things: how organizations work with their people and how those people work together.

## EMPOWERMENT

To succeed, organizations will need to tap into the power of their people in new ways. It is no longer the case that we can train employees and then monitor their performance, tuning execution. We need to align them to a purpose, empower them with the freedom to pursue their roles, and provide chances for self-improvement (Pink, 2011). The associated requirements make up a successful learning culture.

Self-improvement comes not just from courses, but from mentoring and coaching as well as effective self-learning. As an individual moves from novice to practitioner to expert, we must provide different support. The 70:20:10 framework (Jennings, 2013) shows us that relevant workplace learning happens in many ways besides formal training. The model (and the numbers are indicative, not definitive) reflects workers' beliefs that only 10 percent of workplace knowledge comes from training, 20 percent comes from coaching and mentoring, and 70 percent comes from learning on the job. Focusing only on formal learning leaves roughly 90 percent of learning without facilitation, although there is much we *can* do. Basically, the mastery needed to provide motivation isn't being addressed by organizations, even though it could be.

Employees feel *purpose* in their jobs if a company is going beyond sales to focusing on delivering real value to the customer and to society. One initiative that is exemplary of this focus is a movement called "b-corporations," or benefit corporations, that consider contributions to society and the environment in addition to their pursuit of profit. Such a movement gives employees a company that they can feel good about working for.

*Empowerment* comes after employees have purpose and support in achieving and maintaining mastery, which frees them to achieve the important goals. This doesn't mean complete anarchy, and there is a role for leadership, as Dan Pontefract makes clear in *Flat Army* (2013), where he provides a robust look at the skills required to make such an organization work.

## COMMUNICATION

A concomitant outcome of empowerment is the second necessary component to success, *successful interaction*. Innovation is not simply the product of the individual innovator going away and coming back with a new idea. Instead, books like Stephen Johnson's *Where Good Ideas Come From: The Natural History of Innovation* (2010) and Keith Sawyer's *Group Genius: The Creative Power of Collaboration* (2008) tell us that innovation is the product of creative friction, the interplay between individuals. The organizational culture has to be right, but so, too, do the mechanisms for this interplay.

The goal is to move to a structure that is different from the traditional top-down flow of communication, and instead achieve an open exchange where and when needed. Husband (2013) has coined the term "wirearchy," which he defines as "a dynamic two-way flow of power and authority, based on knowledge, trust, credibility and a focus on results, enabled by interconnected people and technology." Husband emphasizes the necessity of communication and the need for a culture in which individuals can be trusted.

There are needs for both cooperation and collaboration. There are times when providing useful pointers, answering questions, and providing examples are sufficient. Then, there are times when teams must work together to solve problems and communities must work together to keep their practice current with the changes that are occurring.

The Coherent Organization framework (see Figure 5.1), initiated by Harold Jarche and developed by the rest of the members in the Internet Time Alliance, maps the flow of information into and out of the organization as well as between colleagues. The model identifies three separate groups that are connected and coordinated with flows of information.

Working parties are ideally composed of individuals with complementary strengths who are members of their communities of practice and bring their knowledge to bear, but also bring back their reflections on their activities in a "design research approach" to their communities. The communities of practice similarly are monitoring developments in society at large for relevant inputs, while sharing the outcomes of their actions and reflections with others. The dialog within a level is facilitated by interactions between levels.

An increasing awareness of the power of storytelling and the role it plays in effective communication is also taking hold. Stories are not only great ways to provide examples in formal learning, but also ways to communicate corporate values. Our cognitive architectures are aligned with stories, allowing them to be powerful communication channels. The message about the value of uplifting stories found in Jonah Sach's *Winning the Story Wars* (2012) also holds true here, and aligns well with the

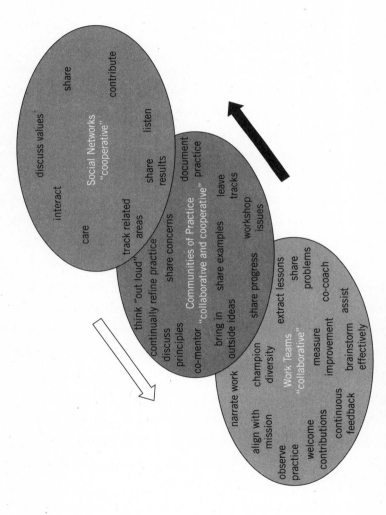

**Figure 5.1** The Coherent Organization

idea of a purpose message. People are motivated by aspiration more than by fear.

My undergraduate thesis was on using email for classroom discussion (circa 1978!). One of the findings my professors and I found were that, with different channels available, people who didn't contribute face-to-face became active in email (and vice versa; Quinn, Mehan, Levin, & Black, 1983). With new social media, we have a variety of ways for people to communicate, and we enrich the opportunities for individuals to contribute.

Increasingly, we are recognizing that communication includes "working out loud." I have long advocated "learning out loud" and, when redefining learning in the broad sense, this also includes working out loud. The benefits include better cycles of communication (leading to continual improvement) and capture of tacit knowledge, reducing organizational vulnerability to staff turnover.

Another role that is showing up in people working together is the role of curation (e.g., Kelly, 2012). As information flows grow greater, our ability to track all relevant information becomes overwhelming. We used to depend on journalists and librarians to curate information, but a variety of problems with those channels, while not eliminating their value, indicate a more sophisticated strategy is necessary. Increasingly, there's a role for someone to be responsible for following relevant activity and culling from that. It may be emergent in many communities, but should not be left to chance.

New forms of communication and interaction also provide new affordances (capabilities) to support action. These new capabilities support new forms of interaction and new outcomes. These opportunities provide a way for individuals to collaborate in achieving organizational goals, if they are willing and able.

## CULTURE

The issue of culture is paramount. The elements together comprise an organization that can continually learn. Let me be clear that "learning" here has a slightly different connotation than you might be familiar with. Learning in this context is more than just training or more than courses. If you are solving a new problem, designing a new system, or conducting research on new technologies and processes when the results aren't known, this larger definition of *learning* is what we need to achieve.

Garvin, Edmondson, and Gino (2008) proposed a suite of elements necessary for an organization that can learn (see Figure 5.2). At core were the elements of a safe environment: making it safe to contribute, valuing diversity, having a real openness to new ideas, and providing time for reflection. In addition, being concrete about learning and having active support from leadership were necessary.

This type of organization can be difficult for leadership to support. Many times, leaders may not trust their workers, either their intelligence or their motivation. I witnessed a situation when management was installing a new organization-wide IT solution, but asked the vendor to turn off the email function, as they didn't want their employees wasting time socializing. These people had phones! Now, this was in the 1980s, but doesn't that feel short-sighted now? It's the same with other social systems.

Many organizations will fail on some of these tests. If you hear "That's not how we do it here," that person is really not

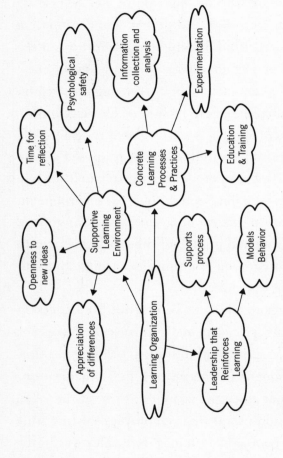

**Figure 5.2  A Learning Organization**
Adapted from Garvin, Edmondson, and Gino, *Harvard Business Review*, March 2008.

54

open to new ideas. If anything you say can and will be used against you, is it really safe to contribute? Culture is not trivial. It's been said that "culture eats strategy for breakfast." The fact is that the finest intentions can be undermined by a legacy culture that's not aligned. Change is hard, but necessary.

Again and again, what emerges is the necessity for people to engage with each other. Dan Pontefract, in *Flat Army* (2013), provides a detailed model of leadership needed to get there, with a key theme of *being open*. The future of organizational success will come from people communicating with each other across the organization, not up and down the hierarchy. This is not or should not be scary, if you trust your people and are open with them yourself. If you don't trust them, nothing else is going to work either, in the long term.

## BOTTOM LINE

- Command and control isn't the path forward.
- Employees need to be given a vision, a mission, and freedom to work.
- Continual innovation comes from creative friction.
- It takes a positive culture for this to work.
- This is an area for L&D responsibility.
- Technology exists that can help.

What tools do we have to hand to help us?

# 6

# Our Technology

In addition to the changes in our understanding of individuals and organizations, we're also seeing changes in the technologies we have to capitalize on. While some of them aren't that new, they have applications in L&D that we're largely not seeing. To take advantage of them, we have to understand them. We have to cut through any hype and ascertain the ways in which these new technologies can be used to support performance.

More importantly, we need to align the technology we use with how we think and perform and how we work and play together. That means reconsidering the technology we use in order to take advantage of new applications that support our performance, our learning, our communication, and our collaboration.

## FORMAL

Technology can augment performance in several ways; in the case of formal learning, technology can enhance what learners experience and also the tools we use to develop experiences and track outcomes. Using the activity-based learning model introduced earlier, in addition to content-delivery and communication tools, we need technology-supported ways for learners to produce outputs and receive information.

Content tools are necessary, but hardly sufficient. The ability to show media to learners, whether text, audio, or video, is a given. Two ways to go beyond this are (1) ways to create meaningful interactions and (2) ways for learners to create and share their own media. The first is really a bare minimum; clearly, learners should have more meaningful learning experiences than answering knowledge questions. Learners also must have access to resources, whether in courses via an LMS or a portal.

Beyond media presentation, we need ways to have learners perform. This starts with simple questions—true/false, multiple-choice, and multi-answer (regardless of interaction mode, drag/drop and matching really boil down to those)—but goes further. Tools such as the ubiquitous "convert content to elearning" solutions can support meaningful interactions, but too often do not.

Beyond such tools, however, we do have tools that actually let you develop meaningful interactions. Branching scenarios model the world and allow learners to interact and explore options, with some limitations. Both specialty tools and the richer authoring environments will support such interactions. Simulation-driven interactions (which, when "tuned" to achieve engagement, become serious games) can provide ability-based adaptation and variability that supports what is essentially infinite replay. For formal learning, this is ideal, as serious games are the next best thing to mentored live performance (which can be more costly and doesn't scale well). However, there are not yet effective tools short of full programming environments to build them (and fundamentally there may never be).

Virtual worlds provide a 3D immersion capability that also typically provides a persistent space that retains knowledge of your previous visits. Benefits beyond the inherent spatial capability include the ability to bridge distance and to choose your own personal appearance (avatar). The overhead is still high, however, both in learning curve and in technical requirements. The initial excitement over virtual worlds masked the challenges, but the long-term benefits, both social and spatial, still provide opportunities for better learning outcomes. Naturally, spatial domains, such as complex physical plants and molecular structures, where social interaction is also beneficial, make good niches for such technology.

Having learners create media is a second valuable way in which they can engage in designed interactions. Having learners create work products, such as documents, audio files, or videos, is one way to capture their thinking. Similarly, documenting processes, doing interviews, or capturing real performance is an excellent media creation activity. Learners can also capture their own performances through interpersonal interactions. To use this method, there is a need for media portals that allow creating and hosting resources.

Social support for learning also is key. The same tools used for social interaction can be used for this purpose. One tendency is to graft such tools onto the LMS. While this makes sense in a business delivering education, for organizations it does not. Social should extend beyond the course and become the hub of learning as learners progress beyond novices. Having separate social platforms for formal learning and organizational communication creates a barrier to migrating between the two. Using the corporate platform to support the formal learning is a more natural segue between the two.

The role of the LMS is changing, too. An effort coming out of the Advanced Distributed Learning initiative of the U.S. Department of Defense has developed a simpler yet richer standard for tracking more than just content delivery. The Experience API (xAPI for short) is a simple syntax for reporting on activities people accomplish (see Table 6.1). This is just a rough example and much finer granularity can be tracked.

Anything that people do through a system can be instrumented and tracked (and things outside the system can be logged as well). Such tracking enables a number of valuable outcomes, including richer suites of activities aggregating as learning experiences, tracking of performance support usage, and noting social contributions.

**Table 6.1**   xAPI Syntax

| Syntax\ Example | \<person\> | \<verb\> | \<activity\> |
|---|---|---|---|
| 1: | \<Chris\> | \<read\> | *\<Engaging Learning\>* |
| 2: | \<Drew\> | \<completed\> | *\<Virtual Leader\>* |
| 3: | \<Pat\> | \<used\> | \<Mentoring Checklist\> |
| 4: | \<Casey\> | \<accessed\> | \<Product XYZ Troubleshooting Checklist\> |

Such enablement isn't sufficient alone, and an associated development is Learning Record Stores (LRS), which arguably should be something more like Experience Record Stores, a richer depiction of individual activity. Such systems, particularly when coupled with business intelligence systems, can provide the foundation for measuring more important outcomes than cost/seat time.

Obviously, the social extensions to formal learning and the xAPI take us beyond formal learning. What else is to hand?

## PERFORMANCE SUPPORT

Performance support is seeing a resurrection. Although decades old now, since Gloria Gery first pointed us in this direction in her *Electronic Performance Support Systems* (1991), the uptake has been slow. However, as economic conditions have tightened and competition has stiffened, organizations have become more open to investigating alternative approaches with higher returns such as performance support (PS).

The point is to deliver solutions at the moment of need, instead of having to break away from the workflow to find them. Resources can now be "to hand." When we recognize how we really perform, the possibility of putting more information in the world is not only viable, but imperative. A performance support focus is a better starting point for organizations than courses!

Checklists have proven valuable at the right moment, as have job aids, decision support, product information, troubleshooting guides—the list goes on. We can provide support before, during, and after events to both make the performance better *and* to turn experiences into learning events. We also have a rich suite of media to draw upon, including documents (text and graphics), audio, video, and interactives. All can be delivered at will.

We now have the technology to insert content into the workflow. It can be embedded in applications, whether by initial design or after the fact, float along above web-delivered solutions, and even travel with us.

Most interestingly, we can now trigger such support by contextual need. With regular software, we can know where a performer is in a process and provide specific guidance. Using sensors, mobile devices can know where we are and what we are doing and provide specific help.

We also have the ability to host such resources in flexible ways customized by a variety of filters and supported by robust search engines. Too often portals are organized by the provider's mindset instead of by good information architecture that supports multiple browsing schemas as well as advanced searching. We can even provide customized suites by role. The problem of siloed content can be addressed with custom interfaces that pull varied resources together into personalized portals.

We have rich ways to provide support at the moment of need. The challenge is for us to take advantage of it.

## SOCIAL

A real revolution in social tools has taken place. Although tools like blogs, wikis, and more are not new, they are still underused in organizations, even though they are capable of providing large opportunities. The new needs of organizations make these tools critical going forward. Use cases for each of the tools have documented business uses in industry; these capabilities need to be leveraged for learning as well.

When we consider the benefits of social learning, we must realize that external viewpoints are likely to include perspectives and information not entirely in synch with the original. By incorporating other viewpoints, the outcome is likely to be richer (Quinn, 2009). This is true for formal learning when we resolve differing viewpoints and generate new ideas or solve problems, the bigger picture of learning.

A caveat: the room is smarter than the smartest person in the room *if you manage the process right.* If not, the room might be only as smart as the most dominant person in the room or the one with the most authority. Research shows, for example, that groups with members possessing high social sensitivity and equal turn-sharing are better at intelligence tasks (and the overall intelligence of the group isn't a correlate; Wooley & Malone, 2011).

This notion of user-generated content is the basis of the claim that the web has evolved from Web 1.0, or producer-generated content, to Web 2.0, or user-generated content. In the early days of the web, only those who could master or pull together a team that could handle the syntax, navigate the directories, and send codes to update the infrastructure could populate the web. Smart folks subsequently made web applications that made it possible for anyone who could master three things—a username, password, and an URL—to put up text, then pictures, and now video and more. Thus, a new era was born in which anyone (and pretty much everyone) could populate the web.

One of the interesting phenomena is still the "shiny new object" syndrome. While these new tools have unique capabilities, we tend to forget that some familiar tools still have use. Email is a social medium, and discussion boards are often underused. It is convenient to have communications (or at least notifications thereof) come into a familiar channel, rather than having to check a variety of different channels. On the flip side, the overuse of "reply all," for instance, has made email less than optimal and often aversive. Still, there are times when email or discussion lists are the best solution, such as for asynchronous conversations. They support both formal and informal learning as a channel for dialog and debate.

Blogs (the term derives from a shortening of "web logs," essentially online journals) are ways to share reflections in ways that others can contribute to. Blogs provide a richer medium for communication than, say, microblogs, and support more reflective communication. Reflection is one of those elements that is underappreciated, yet it adds considerable benefit when used. Beyond formal learning, blogs can be a way for a leader to communicate to followers or for teams to communicate progress.

Microblogs typically support shorter communications, more often pointers to interesting references or questions. Unlike instant messaging (also valuable at times), microblogs go to anyone who's paying attention to (following) a person. This can be a synchronous channel for supplementing conversation (e.g., in a classroom or presentation) or asynchronous to share information or request assistance.

The choice of who to follow on blogs and microblogs can be facilitated by seeing who else is following certain people. You may have to spend some time sorting through folks who don't add value, but you should find others, internally or externally, who are providing value in their posts. Interestingly, if someone you admire both microblogs (usually through Twitter, known as "tweeting") and blogs, by following what he or she finds interesting and his or her reflections, you can use the person as a model of thinking. The person can serve as a mentor and not even know it! I call this "stealth mentoring."

Instant messaging or chat can be valuable as well. Typically limited to a particular group instead of supporting everyone who wants to follow, this exclusivity can be beneficial for more private conversations. Supporting continual conversations in a more informal mechanism than email, with discrete channels, the value is for small teams to communicate on topic.

Wikis, the original term for shared documents, are well established as a collaborative tool in some areas, but have yet to penetrate more broadly. Far more efficient than emailing documents back and forth for revision, wikis can track contributions and often support conversations alongside the documents. It is true (and this is changing) that the capabilities fall short of the rich capabilities available in dedicated document processing programs. Still, working collaboratively on documents, whether for formal learning assignments or work deliverables, capitalizes on the benefits of multiple contributors and facilitates the quality of thought.

For both work teams and communities, the capabilities of collective intelligence offer improved outcomes. Sharing solutions are now available from the purveyors of document processing solutions. Whether collaborating first and then polishing or working in a rich environment to begin with (still embryonic and not without hiccups), the benefits to collaborative generation trump the problems with version control that exist with handoffs.

## MOBILE

Not surprisingly, mobile is now a given. The uptake of devices is at such a rate that the developed world has reached saturation (more subscriptions than subscribers, as many individuals have more than one device), and the developing world is booming. The potential for mobile to facilitate L&D is considerable (Quinn, 2011).

The devices, ranging from pocketables (smart phones and even the new forms of PDA, such as Apple's iPod Touch) through tablets, are showing up everywhere, whether provided by the organization or "bring your own device" (BYOD). As an aside, laptops are generally not considered mobile devices (my own definition stipulates that the device has to be naturally usable in two hands with no support), but when doing something contextually relevant they may qualify.

The natural use of these devices includes augmenting formal learning, providing performance support, and accessing community. These are not unique to mobile, but having that capability anywhere and anytime is a major benefit.

A unique advantage of mobile is the ability to provide contextually specific information, as indicated for performance support, discussed above. The sensors in mobile devices can pinpoint where a device is or which way it's pointing or how it's being held, as well as capturing visual and auditory data. New sensors exist or are coming out, including atmospheric pressure, temperature, and potentially more.

The small(er) screens of mobile devices, more constrained interfaces, and more limited processors and requirements on battery life do provide some barriers to fulfilling their full potential, but existing devices do possess powerful capability to deliver meaningful support. Cross-platform lack of compatibility also has provided some barriers. However, the tools are becoming ever richer, the devices are ever more powerful, and the interfaces are yielding new opportunities almost daily. The fact of the matter is that mobile is here to stay and ready for primetime.

Two intriguing extensions to predictable mobile capability are augmented and alternate reality games. Each of these provides uniquely valuable learning and performance opportunities.

Augmented reality is when technology adds additional information into the current context, such as taking in the scene via camera, layering on additional information, and presenting that information through the screen. Audio can also be contextually delivered. An example is Yelp, a tool that provides information about businesses. For example, you can search for restaurants wherever you are. The baseline is telling the program where you are and asking for a type of business (e.g., a restaurant) near you. If the device is equipped with a global positioning system chipset (GPS), the device can actually pinpoint you on a map and show where the restaurants are relative to you. If the device has a compass and a camera, you can hold up the device and it will layer on the picture of where you're looking with which restaurants are in that direction!

This capability has clear implications for supporting performance. Imagine looking around a physical plant and seeing the complex machinery labeled as to function, fixing a machine and having the parts labeled and the directions to push or pull a piece to remove/replace it, or investigating a new office park and finding out about the businesses there.

Alternate reality games (ARGs) are different. They are like typical serious games in that there's a story line and the player has decisions to make, but instead of playing inside a simulated world, the situation emulates and penetrates the real world. You might have to answer a particular phone or pick up a newspaper at a particular location or respond to emails and texts as the story plays out.

A real-world example was the I Love Bees game used as a promotion for a new release of the computer game Halo. Websites were discovered via clues that indicated a business that ultimately was under alien espionage, and players around the world had to piece together puzzles and coordinate actions to figure out and stop the insidious plot.

Again, this has valuable implications for learning. As Koreen Olbrish Pagano's book *Immersive Learning* points out (2013), such experiences, designed to embed learning decisions in context, support a rich and very real practice environment.

## INFRASTRUCTURE

Mobile brings up another interesting area. One of the advances that is making content more accessible is the emerging standard of HTML 5 (Katz, 2010). This syntax, supporting both content and interaction, provides a broadly implemented support infrastructure that crosses platforms. It makes implementing easier, but it takes a more structured approach to content development, which can serve as a catalyst for needed change in content.

An element that has been taking hold in commercial web projects is becoming viable for L&D. Advanced web systems are now developing content, not by handcrafting such experiences, but by pulling from databases by rule-driven behavior based on context. Such systems provide greater governance over content development and more flexibility in content delivery (Quinn, 2012a, 2012b).

The concept is to develop content into models that add definition around the components. For example, with formal learning you could define components for introductions, concepts, examples, and so on. The benefits of decoupling is that content now can be delivered to meet different needs, in different contexts, on different devices. Thus, a learning example could be accessed separately for help in solving a particular problem, or a concept could be accessed to diagnose a defect.

Further, such efforts reduce redundancy when implemented across silos. For example, instead of the same marketing materials being repurposed by separate groups for sales training, customer training, and customer support, the content could be developed in a way that populates the needs for all groups.

The content is also written in a way that separates how it looks from what it says. eXtensible Markup Language (or XML) supports this, and tools for content built on this system, such as Darwin Integrated Topic Architecture (DITA), have become an industry-wide standard for content. The support available around these standards minimizes the pain and risk associated with such a separation.

Coupled with architectures that allow accessing content by description instead of location, such systems support customization and personalization of information. With these mechanisms, content can be pulled up by asking for pieces that match a set of parameters, such as in this vertical market, this type of content, and more. So one could ask for the video example that used the financial services context when dealing with negotiation.

These processes also can be automated so that business rules are used to match user to context to content. Such systems are being seen in commercial web applications. If you've ever had Amazon or Netflix make a recommendation, where they see your choice and suggest you might also like some other item, this isn't being done by someone individually watching your transaction (an approach that would be impossible to staff), but data and rules are used to characterize your interests, match yours to those of others, and bring up recommendations.

The result is Web 3.0, system-generated content, also known as the Semantic Web. Web 3.0 will be increasingly valuable for organizations, not only for their customer-facing experiences, but also for internally facing learning, development, and performance needs. The core is the use of semantics, or tags, that describe the content. The addition of these descriptors is a seemingly trivial extension, but the potential outcomes are significant. The ability to pull content by description supports customization by device and context, enabling mobile as well as personalization to individuals by knowledge, experience, role, preferences, and more.

Robert Glushko's *The Discipline of Organizing* (2013) is a deep treatment of the necessary rigor in information science needed for the semantic approach. The structural and definitional systematicity required is considerable, but the support for content governance and flexible delivery offer large benefits. The power of customization is just beginning to be seen.

An additional outcome of robust infrastructure and the xAPI is the ability to generate a fine granularity of activity across an enterprise, creating a large set of valuable data. While the buzzword is "big data," or analytics, the real value is the insight to be found by examining that data. By coupling usage data with other data sets in the enterprise documenting key business intelligence, examiners can find out what resources and actions contribute to organizational success. This data provides a means to identify areas to address, track the effectiveness of interventions, and document impact.

It is still early for such an infrastructure, but the need already exists. Fortunately, tools such as content management systems and tagging schemes exist. Coupled with the xAPI for tracking, we can explore the access of content, understand the impact on effectiveness, and fine-tune our systems for optimal performance. We can, and should, enable robust infrastructures to support next-generation content capabilities.

## BOTTOM LINE

- We have tools to create meaningful formal learning experiences.
- We have the ability to deliver necessary performance support.
- We have the systems to support important interpersonal interaction.
- We have the tools to track rich learning experiences.

*(Continued)*

- We can bring content pretty much anywhere we need it.

- We can customize what we bring for the right person, at the right time, in the right way, on the right device.

The tools are there. As Arthur C. Clarke famously said, "Any suitably advanced technology is indistinguishable from magic" (1984). We're there. We have magic, so the question is: What we are going to do with it? What are the integrated elements, and what would an enlightened and enabled L&D look like?

# SECTION 3

# ALIGNING

To move forward, we need to characterize an approach. We need a framework for thinking about making changes. We need some principles that guide us in integrating our learning, organizations, and technology. We need to understand what an enabled organization would look like. And we will benefit from some case studies.

# 7

# A Framework
# for Moving Forward

We would benefit from a framework to characterize different areas that comprise L&D activities. Over the course of a number of my engagements with organizations looking to become more strategic in the use of technology to support achieving performance, a pattern emerged (Quinn, 2009). This pattern covers the various elements that constitute the full spectrum of opportunities to support learning outcomes (see Figure 7.1). The focus of the model is on coupling the elements together to yield an integrated solution for performance covering both optimal execution and continual innovation.

While initially used to consider elearning, this exploration of the elements of a performance ecosystem applies more broadly to L&D strategy. The notion of integrating formal learning, performance support, and social learning, then considering the successful integration through infrastructure and

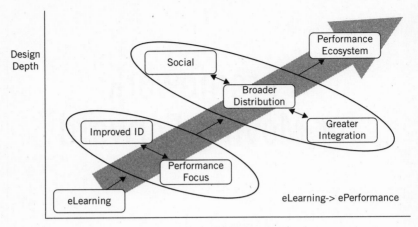

**Figure 7.1** eLearning Strategy

focus, provides a broader perspective on the human-centered activities that support both execution and innovation.

Entry to technology typically includes initial elearning (putting content on the web with a quiz or a virtual classroom), performance support via portals and/or knowledge management, or social media supporting eCommunity. A step forward in terms of formal learning is advanced instructional design for elearning, creating learning experiences not just courses. The use of more flexible designs to support cross-platform delivery achieves a broader reach, and tighter back-end integration supports efficiencies and new capabilities. The goal is the integration of the elements into a user-centered ecosystem with the focus on supporting work, not on the different business units that contribute.

This framework has proved to be a viable mechanism to assess progress and to guide strategy. Whether in workshops

**Table 7.1** Elements of Strategy

| Category | Principle | Approach |
| --- | --- | --- |
| Culture | Empower | Experimentation |
| Formal | Proprietary Only | Serious |
| Performance Focus | Support When Justified | Least Assistance Principle |
| Social | Default | Facilitation |
| Infrastructure | Content Model | Semantics |
| Metrics | Business Impact | Instrument and Analytics |

or engagements, understanding the elements and their role has helped organizations determine what priorities to ascribe in the near, mid, and long term. Underpinning this way of looking at aligning strategy is the culture that these efforts fit in and the metrics used to achieve and evaluate success. If we take the components of culture, formal, performance support, social, infrastructure, and metrics, we can create overarching principles and approaches for each of these areas as a guide (see Table 7.1).

For culture, the focus has to move from controlling to empowering. Organizations need to be looking at how to motivate with meaningful work, and support both in immediate ways in the moment and over time. It has to be safe and valuable to contribute. The approach is to continually experiment and refine ways to augment human capabilities with technology support to create a vibrant problem-solving environment, and build a culture *of experimentation*.

Formal learning has to not regenerate work others can provide, but instead focus on unique differentiators for the organization. If it's off the shelf or if pre-existing resources are sufficient, the organization can focus on elements that are particular to its success, even to the point of focusing only on culture and on learning to learn and work together. The approach has to be a serious approach to learning, providing sufficient practice to actually achieve change. This does not preclude humor and engagement (to the contrary), but does mean that any formal learning will be sufficiently resourced.

For a performance focus, support should be used as often as justifiable, with a strong emphasis on putting information in the world. It should not be assumed that support is needed, but the option should be examined prior to resorting to courses. When used, support should be tested and tuned to achieve the desired outcomes. This should mean a minimalist approach (Carroll, 1990), leveraging the knowledge of the individual and the context to provide only the information necessary to get back to work. Think about it as the "Least Assistance Principle" (Quinn, 2011), where you answer the question "What's the *least* I can do to guide the performance?" Perhaps counterintuitive to the L&D mindset, this approach is actually preferred by individuals who need to perform a task. A small allowance of extra development to link the recommended and supported performance to concepts that guide performance is allowed if used to develop a performer's understanding and ability to adapt to new and changing circumstances.

Social should become the default solution for meeting learning and development needs. With vibrant communities of practice and work teams, connected to each other and the broader Internet, solutions should exist for self-help via the network. As things move faster, the likelihood of having time to codify a solution or chances that the situation won't be unique have decreased. As a consequence, individuals will either be uncovering existing answers, collaboratively solving problems, or accessing experts, then creating their own answers. The approach will be facilitating the process, rather than owning the solution.

Behind the user-facing elements is the infrastructure. While integrating systems to create a coherent ecosystem is also part of that infrastructure, the focus should be on providing more structure around the underpinning elements. With that effort to make content more structured (and consequently more flexible) comes an emphasis on semantics. The integration of meaning-tagged content and rule-driven access provides the ability to start delivering contextualized and personalized support. Mobile naturally falls out of this effort, but is an infrastructure consideration.

Finally, L&D has to be aligned with metrics that matter to the organization. Addressing efficiency in lieu of impact is meaningless. The data that should matter are deltas on customer satisfaction and secondary metrics like sales, errors, time to troubleshoot, and so forth. We must instrument far more than courses, using elements like the xAPI to have a rich picture of what's happening and analytics to address intended outcomes and mine for unintended insights.

This is not merely a hypothetical model. There is evidence that investment in learning and development provides benefits not only on specific metrics but on overall organizational performance. Two separate studies (Bassi, McGraw, & McMurrer, 2004; Overton & Dixon, 2013) demonstrate the potential benefits.

Bassi and her colleagues cite a number of cases pointing to the conclusion that companies that invest in good human capital return greater shareholder value. They evaluated company investment in their people and compared that to business success. They concluded that investing in culture has a financial payoff.

In the second study, Overton and Dixon, from Towards Maturity, an organization that promotes advanced learning technology strategy to yield business benefits, used a framework of component levels of improvement, vetted through expert review, to benchmark companies (see Appendix B). In their 2013 report, they found that learning groups that rate highly against their benchmarks also report improvements. Measurable improvements, for example, are found in the ability to change product lines or processes, higher customer satisfaction ratings, and increased productivity (Overton & Dixon, 2013).

The framework presented in this chapter characterizes the space for opportunity in organizations wishing to move forward.

## BOTTOM LINE

- We need to be strategic.
- Our strategy needs to integrate formal, performance support, and social.
- Our strategy needs to incorporate culture, infrastructure, and metrics.
- There are real business benefits to be achieved.

How does this work?

# 8

# What Does This Look Like?

**G**iven what we have in hand, what would an effective L&D effort look like? In this chapter, we explore perspectives and case studies and allow you to self-assess your current status.

## STAKEHOLDER PERSPECTIVES

One way to look at the topic is through different perspectives: employee, manager, executive, and, of course, the L&D perspective.

### Employee Perspective

Jordan and Casey hit the ground running as new hires on the same day, but they differ considerably. Jordan comes into a customer-facing position with essentially zero experience, while Casey is an experienced engineer. Both were connecting with others before their first day on campus, with engaging experiences that helped to develop their understanding of the company culture. They were introduced to the company tools via goal-based simulations and chose communities and created a community profile to be available from the first day. Jordan, however, was also introduced to the basics of customer service through experiential learning that was grounded in Jordan's own experience as a consumer, and to the company's specific approaches via scenarios.

They reach the endgame of the alternate reality experience that introduced them to the company when they arrive. They use the information and the physical plant to put together information that lets them accomplish a goal that also cements their understanding of the company and puts them at the location of the brief on-boarding. The on-boarding reinforces the messages sent earlier about what matters to the company, focusing on culture, mission, and vision. After some initial orientation time and connecting with other new hires, they're off to meet with their managers for a conversation about expectations, mentoring and coaching, ongoing projects and to be officially introduced to the team.

Casey will be in a co-mentoring situation with Taylor, another engineer with less overall experience but more experience at the company. This will help Taylor learn more about engineering, while Casey can get up to speed on the way the company operates. Jordan will be given some coached interactions with customers, until mutual agreement is reached on achieving an acceptable level of performance.

In addition to meeting their teammates, Casey and Jordan will meet members of the communities they have joined. Whether live or virtually, they will have a chance to learn about the basic resources of the community and any ongoing or special events. Casey's experience provides a leg up into the community, while Jordan may take some time to be active.

Jordan is joined at a workstation by Pat and is walked through a series of live calls, with a reflection period after each. While Jordan could work remotely, an introductory period for meeting team members and being steeped in the culture of the company is considered a valuable investment. When Jordan's ready, Pat steps back and becomes available on an as-needed basis, while continually monitoring Jordan and the team for opportunities to improve.

Both Jordan and Casey will follow the blog and microblog posts of their managers. By so doing, they're better aligned with the mission as well as seeing how the next level in the organization thinks.

Casey hits the ground running, launched into a project team with a clear deliverable and with Casey's prior experience providing complementary skills. The team is aware of Casey's background and leverages Casey's skills, while providing an entry path into the organization's vocabulary and processes. Between the pre-work and the team's support, Casey's contributing in a meaningful way in a short period of time.

Both Jordan and Casey find a digital work environment that contains a one-click access to their network, both work team and community, and a suite of resources "to hand." The resources may have been developed by one of the communities of practice or L&D, if they're proprietary to the company, or are likely to be curated by either. These resources include a variety of modalities, including static text and diagrams for step-by-step procedures, audio files for hands-free use, videos for contextualized support, and interactives for mixed-initiative dialogs.

Casey is immediately thrust into using collaborative documents to develop deliverables, both reading to get up to speed and then adding to them via comments and editing. Jordan uses existing resources, including team-developed FAQs, scripts, and decision trees, but also can identify parameters within which there is flexibility to adapt. An advisor is always on tap. A clear focus on the outcome of customer satisfaction guides Jordan's performance. Eventually, Jordan will be helping develop new scripts.

The resources are available in a portal that is customized by role for the user, not by the business unit responsible. The portal is searchable as well, and embedded in the community. For instance, Jordan and Casey will be expected to continue to monitor their own sources, integrate what's found, and share relevant elements. Resources are rated by users and proactively offered. The range of offerings runs from performance support through quick modules, to full courses. The resources coming out of work teams and communities are collaboratively developed and maintained. Governance for all content is distributed, but ensured.

When Jordan and Casey are on the go, the resources are still available via a mobile portal. Some of the resources will adapt for mobile usage, whether simplifying for the context or reformatting. Further, some will offer contextualized help, and other contextualized resources may appear. There are mobile-specific support apps as well.

Both Jordan and Casey will be more tightly coupled to their own performance. They will have the ability, and the responsibility, to track how they are doing. The elements to be included will emphasize intangibles like contributions, rather than just measuring effort. The emphasis is on self-improvement, rather than on comparisons and compensation.

Jordan and Casey will occasionally still take courses, but they're going to be available when a significant skill shift is needed, such as new processes or tools, and they'll be very minimal in scope. There will be a big emphasis on learning together and/or significant practice. Unless the material is proprietary or has a unique organizational spin, the courses will be curated from outside or outsourced, even for new initiatives.

Overall, the focus is on empowering employees by giving them clear goals and the partners and tools to succeed. Jordan and Casey are expected both to call on the network as needed and to contribute when appropriate.

## Manager Perspective

Jordan's leader is Pat. Pat has the same sort of support for working, but her tasks are different. Pat's job is to set the direction for the team in alignment with the unit's overall mission as set by the executive overseeing customer relations, Drew. Pat empowers the team and supports them in achieving their goals while removing barriers. Pat will use a dashboard to track activity, but with a view to finding opportunities to improve the group's performance. That may include helping the team focus, reviewing processes for improvement (with the team's input), and identifying skill gaps for intervention.

Drew will assign Pat to assist some teams working on forward-looking tasks. This helps Pat meet others with valuable insights and complementary skills and helps to leverage Pat's abilities in service of organizational goals. This reciprocal exchange creates valuable inputs to the organization as well as developing Pat.

The main tool in Pat's repertoire is coaching and mentoring. While Pat can call on L&D to point to some commercial resources for specific skills, Pat's role is more to identify skill gaps and try for a minimalist mechanism for addressing them, particularly through small challenges and reflection sessions for Jordan and other team members. Pat has a coaching checklist and a mentoring guide for use as needed, to support the best decisions, and similarly has Drew on call as well.

Pat's development, consequently, is focused on creating an awareness of customer service skills and the associated interventions. Similarly, Pat is a member of several communities, including first-level leadership, coaching, mentoring, and customer service management. Pat came onboard with a mix of service and leadership skills and has been similarly developed in those areas by mentors in communities.

Pat is open about vision and methods. Pat regularly blogs on team directions and strategy and points to things that emerge as interesting via the corporate microblog. Altogether, Pat leaves a trail of thought that team members like Jordan can use to self-mentor (or stealth mentor). Pat happily gives and shares credit, knowing that the success of team members means Pat is succeeding.

### Executive Perspective

In addition to duties assessing the direction of customer relations, Drew keeps an eye on Pat and the other managers, checking their activity, assessing their alignment, and looking for opportunities to assist them in improving their abilities to communicate with their team members.

Members of Drew's communities will mentor Drew. In the organization strategy community, another executive and Drew will co-mentor on ideas. In leadership, a member of the leadership community with more experience guides Drew in higher-level thinking.

Drew participates in several work teams that are initiated by the CEO, working with others who provide different viewpoints and complementary skills. Such tasks provide top-level insight to the organization and develop all of the participants' strategic skills.

Similarly, Drew mentors Pat and the other managers in a customer service leadership community. Input from the community helps shape the strategy and improves alignment. Drew blogs and microblogs as well, to share and develop the managers.

Drew is continually pleased to see the quality of input from the teams and managers. The impact of these inputs substantially increases the performance of the unit, and Drew is well aware of the strategic role L&D plays. Drew is on the L&D governance board, given the core focus of the organization on customer satisfaction, and is involved in overseeing L&D work in continually enhancing the capability of the infrastructure, facilitating the ongoing communication, and backstopping operations with performance support—and even courses, when needed. The direct impact on customer satisfaction is made manifest through tracking of L&D activities and mapping to impact, and not just for Drew's group.

## L&D Perspective

Chris led the charge for the reorganization of L&D and has had to preside over a shift. Most of the folks working for Chris have been supported in transitioning to a new job. They were not laid off, but instead reskilled to be focusing on different ways of supporting individuals in the organization. The goal has shifted from running courses to facilitating performance in every way.

The tools being used now are social networks and performance support portals, primarily. Courses are secondary, whether run in a classroom or online. More importantly, the courses are not delivered as an "event," but are extended across time and media to create learning experiences that truly develop learners' ability to perform with skill and confidence.

No one has the title "trainer." When one of Chris's team is facilitating a course, his or her role is not to present the content, but to explain activities, provide support for accessing relevant resources, and facilitate conversations and reflection.

That facilitation role continues across social interactions, in teams and communities. A significant portion of those working for Chris will be looking for those who are not effective enough in communicating, using tools, and contributing. Chris's team is playing a governance role on communities and work teams, too, looking for evidence of ongoing improvement and interactions incoming and outgoing. One person from Chris's team is specifically looking at part of Drew's organization, including Pat and the team, including Jordan.

Another role is curating and creating job support resources. Whether internally created or external, a member of Chris's team will be looking for opportunities for which job tasks are requiring support for comprehensibility or quality. The team will also be supporting individuals in teams or communities in creating resources, editing, rewriting, and developing.

A critical responsibility for Chris is monitoring the company culture. Whatever culture the organization has chosen, there should be alignment between how people interact and what is purported to be valuable.

An important component of those working for Chris will be ongoing experimentation with new techniques and tools. The team needs to lead the charge on testing and refining working processes that extend thinking and problem solving. Continual innovation will be the new normal, and optimal execution will be a background assumption.

## CASE STUDIES

Going beyond the ideal, we can look at attempts to initiate change within organizations. Here is a suite of individuals with foresight on the way things can and should go and their efforts to achieve improvements.

Not all the situations are ideal, as there is not adequate support in each instance all the way up the chain, so, consequently, not all the outcomes are optimal. Yet the insights to be gained are valuable. Each has his or her own way to communicate, and it is important to let them tell their own stories.

## MARK BRITZ

I first heard of Mark Britz when he was talking about social in ways that resonated with our thoughts in the Internet Time Alliance. I subsequently tracked him from his previous position to his new opportunity to establish learning at Systems Made Simple and have come to respect the thoughtful way he puts into practice the principles he articulates. He shares with us his story of starting with an open slate.

## What Are Your Organization's Characteristics?

Systems Made Simple (SMS) is a privately owned Healthcare IT company with concentrated attention on government contract work (primarily in health care clinical and delivery systems at the Department of Veterans Affairs, Military Health Systems, and the Department of Health and Human Services). SMS specializes in four core areas of competency: Program and Project Management; System and Software Engineering; Infrastructure Management; and IT Services. SMS uses an extended workforce model. With roughly 450 employees working on more than forty contracts, we work closely with partners and subcontractors to ensure the right talent mix is in place to meet the customer's needs. SMS is geographically dispersed throughout the United States, with offices in Syracuse, New York, Vienna, Virginia, Salt Lake City, Utah, Austin, Texas, and Clearwater, Florida. Our project teams include a mix of employees who work from home, in government facilities, or in SMS offices.

The workforce is not only extended by time and geography, but also by function and relationship to the organization. Most SMS employees are accustomed to working closely with other project team members to function as a single, cohesive team as seen by the customer. While a large number of employees are hired for direct contractual work, the intention is to provide career growth opportunities for each employee. Our employees are more often experts and practitioners, not novices. They are well versed in their craft, often coming to us with a wealth of experience.

## What Situation Did You Come Into?

SMS was started in 1991 with an initial focus on private-sector development and support projects. In 2002, the company shifted its focus to U.S. government contracts, with an emphasis on the needs of the Department of Veterans Affairs. After winning several larger proposals in the subsequent years, the workforce quickly increased to include partners and subcontractors. Communication and performance consistency became a critical need. More attention was placed on infrastructure (technical and human) to support rapid growth in business development and execution. With these needs mounting, the SMS executive team decided to add a more formal learning function in 2012.

## What Is Your Strategic Plan?

Needing little in the area of formal training and more support for continuous learning in an agile work environment, the company decided from the onset to focus on social and informal learning at the center, rather than a formal first approach. A 70:20:10 "SMS Corporate University" concept serves as the backbone for learning and performance. At its center is an Enterprise Social Network (ESN). Learning & Development (L&D) shifts from a traditional role and serves as a community facilitator encouraging peer-to-peer learning within the workflow. To increase the use of collaborative tools, we are employing a "ground cover" strategy, in which we will nurture groups throughout the organization simultaneously within close work-related proximity. To do this, we first created an internal advisory committee with diverse representation to help spread use by identifying "where collaboration exists" and "where it's needed." We place emphasis on building ambassadors who model productive uses of the tools and encourage users.

Communities of practice (CoPs) and mentoring are also a part of the approach. These CoPs and mentoring opportunities are supported asynchronously with the ESN platform. Additionally, L&D serves to facilitate informal (pull) learning rather than create content or events. By guiding subject matter experts (SMEs) in the development of user-generated support materials such as job aids and recordings, SMS is building a robust library of internal resources that better ensures consistency of execution. A proprietary knowledge management (KM) system is being developed and will seamlessly integrate with the ESN. This KM tool will allow all employees to draw from and contribute to more explicit information in the flow of their work and their individual skill sets. The final component is formal training. Sometimes training is needed to fill skill gaps. Leveraging the wisdom of our workforce, we look to identify vendors and architect a portal to access and secure best-of-kind opportunities in online and face-to-face programs.

## How Is It Working?

In a word—slow. Big change is a gradual process. Being "greenfield" and a one-person show means that addressing the traditional expectations of L&D and meeting the immediate needs of the organization can detract from overall strategy execution. The belief in training as the default solution is fading, albeit slowly, as it is well ingrained, as in most settings. However, to date, we have made great advances in user-generated resources for project managers and are now enacting the ESN.

## What Advice Would You Give to Others?

Remember that at the core of organizational learning are people and not content, instruction, or technology. It's about helping them to reduce their challenges and remove barriers in the most pragmatic ways. Change begins with sharing this belief with leadership in the most direct ways and with high frequency. Without committed support to rethinking the approach to organizational learning, you stand little chance of making progress. Expect to move slowly. Identify scalable solutions and share results often and through multiple channels. Stay focused on individual pain points that directly tie to measurable business results. To accelerate adoption of a 70:20:10 framework, more ambassadors from inside and outside of L&D will be needed. Although L&D can fulfill the role of facilitator of formal asset creation by SMEs, it is those outside of L&D who will perpetuate the use of collaborative media to further accelerate the change in belief and practice from "wait to get" to "give and get."

## TULSER

I first met Jos Arets and Vivian Heinjnen at an ASTD International Conference, where they talked clearly about social and performance support. Jos is the chief executive officer of Tulser, and Vivien is the managing director. Subsequent conversations have led to several interactions between Tulser and members of the Internet Time Alliance. Based in the Netherlands, Tulser is an anagram of "result," and they have had a track record of helping organizations achieve just that. Here they present one example of their work, integrating a human performance improvement (HPI) model with other concepts such as 70:20:10.

### What Are the Organization's Characteristics?

The organization provides medical and nursing care and a sheltered environment. To enable their clients to live as independently as possible in their own homes, housework support, home care, and various forms of specialized home nursing and treatment are provided. The organization has many different locations.

## What Situation Did You Come Into?

The organization was strongly centralized with a high level of hierarchy. Workers were not allowed to decide how to deliver the best care and satisfy the needs of clients. Besides this, a stronger regional presence in relation to the care chain partners (hospitals and municipalities) was crucially important in order to make up for the dwindling government funding, to safeguard the continuity of the organization, and to play a meaningful role in the regional first-line care.

Furthermore, there was pressure on the financial results, which threatened to jeopardize continuity in caregiving. It was also important to become attractive as an employer in the region to prevent outflow to competing organizations and to increase the appeal of this labor market as a whole.

Business analyses, performance analyses, and root cause analyses were conducted under the guidance of external consultants. Maximum use was made of the measurement tools that the organization used for management purposes. These tools could then be used again for evaluating the practice. Top management validated and prioritized the analyses on an organizational level.

These analyses determined the following organizational gaps with negative business impact:

- Concern costs are too high;
- Productivity is too low to survive;

- Sickness absenteeism is high;

- Low levels of satisfaction exist among personnel; and

- There's a breakdown of trust in the management by customers, stakeholders, and family doctors.

### What Was Your Strategic Plan?

The design of this practice was reached in co-creation with the CEO, top management, and representatives of the caregivers. With Rummler's Nine-Box Model, a system approach was used to intervene on three dimensions.

Interventions at the organizational and process level:

- Reformulate strategic goals with the implementation of self-directed teams in mind;

- Redesign structure and processes;

- Set up approximately one hundred autonomous, self-directed, local teams; and

- Reduce management.

Interventions at the performer level:

- Innovative (online) work- and learn-scape to support the self-directed teams to network, cooperate, communicate, develop and share knowledge, and learn from and through each other, with the following characteristics:

  - *Performance (HPI method)*. Assessments are consistently performed to determine whether any performance problems are caused by a deficit in competence or organizational barriers. The structure and processes and the output-based steering were, for example, redesigned to facilitate the changeover to a new organizational format. This was a major precondition for the further development of the organization.

- *Continuous co-creation.* The starting point is that co-creation continuously enriches the work- and learnscape, with current and relevant best practices and nice-to-know and need-to-know information.

- *Informal learning with social software.* Social software was used to strengthen informal/formal learning by making effective use of a virtual environment containing contemporary social media tools.

- *Formal and informal learning interventions.* Formal training courses and meetings for informal learning at the workplace to strengthen the organization development program.

- *Mobile performance support.* Working is learning, and with mobile performance support, the professionals are able to perform (critical) tasks.

To support the self-directed teams, the organization moved from traditional training programs to a contemporary connect and collaborate approach of "working is learning." Instead of courses, we provided 24/7 resources and support learning at the workplace level. The 70:20:10 model was used to design learning interventions. That's why the focus was not on training interventions but on supporting self-directed teams at the workplace, including mobile performance support.

## How Did It Work?

The practice changed the behavior of the personnel, the managers, and the support staff. Care is now being increasingly provided in small-scale, self-directed teams and delivered in a more demand-driven setting.

- A different management format is increasing output and creating space for co-creation, bottom-up initiatives, and hence more self-management in the organization;

- Self-directed teams are resulting in new forms of cooperation with the management and the workers (redesign);

- As a result of the practice, 70 to 90 percent of the personnel are working on primary care tasks and on preconditions so that they can operate as self-directed teams (redesign);

- 90 to 100 percent of the teams have adopted a more systematic approach to work meetings and client discussions. This raises efficiency levels and generates initiatives for quantifiable improvements;

- The digital work- and learn-scape has led to more efficient and effective internal coordination (e.g., digital transfer of client information and changes in the rosters);

- 90 to 100 percent of the teams have learned to work with the Plan-Do-Check-Act improvement methodology, with quantifiable results for the organization (HPI-inside approach);

- 90 to 100 percent of managers have reported a significant improvement in internal communication: more feedback, an increase in problem-solving capacity and self-management among the personnel and teams;

- Each self-directed team has made a team improvement plan. These plans show a shift from internal team business to coordination with other teams and support services in the region;

- Managers are steering more clearly on an output basis. The "what" is more clearly defined, so that the teams can give form and content to the "how";

- Managers are facilitating the teams more effectively in terms of organization and preconditions;

- Managers are giving the teams more effective feedback on performance and are using the team dashboard in order to provide them with consistent support in the realization of sustainable improvement;

- The work- and learn-scape was adopted rapidly by the employees of this organization, due to the fact that this seemed to be an effective way of communication and collaboration. Many employees are working remotely and the work- and learn-scape is a 24/7 resource for everyone. Knowledge production and sharing was possible by posting blogs and forum discussions; and

- The platform was used very regularly in employee meetings as a tool for exchanging information and knowledge and was consulted as a source of information for the project. The employees and the managers are very enthusiastic about the possibilities of the platform. This appears to be creating entirely new opportunities for the development of KPIs to measure the effectiveness of educational efforts.

Besides these behavioral changes, the financial revenue was above 2 million Euro in one year. The expectation is that this is just the beginning. Because of the design of the solution, the results will be sustainable.

## What Advice Would You Give to Others?

There are several lessons learned. The most important are

- Always use a results-based approach. We use HPI in a strict manner to guide clients through the change process.

- Start right from the beginning with a blueprint for evaluation. Otherwise, you are always too late to get the right data and mindset.

- Mobile performance support is a contemporary and much-valued means to support the professionals to perform better.

- Make best practices and lessons learned available at the work- and learn-scape.

- Make a change management blueprint for future organizational changes and development. An important element of this blueprint is the continuous involvement of top management from the beginning of each practice.

## JANE BOZARTH

Dr. Jane Bozarth is the elearning coordinator for the North Carolina Office of State Human Resources and in that capacity often consults on training solutions and other interventions. I had the pleasure of getting to know Jane at a variety of conferences and have been impressed by her presentations and wit. A well-known author and speaker, she cuts through hype with a keen sensibility and has helped clear the air around creating presentations and using social media. She is bringing out a new book, *Show Your Work*, resonant with the thoughts expressed elsewhere in this book. Here she was kind enough to detail a government example.

## Background

Some years ago, I came into a small government agency that had no formal training—or trainers—in place. The advantage here is that I didn't have to overcome status quo or "how we've always done it" thinking.

The organization requested help with "implementing a formal training program," although they didn't have much of a definition for that. There was a certain expectation that this would look like someone standing in front of a room talking. The new HR director was concerned about compliance training and new hire orientation not being delivered so wanted to hire a "trainer." These defined needs were not tied to any particular problem, just the HR director's belief that an organization was supposed to have a training department of sorts. There were some vaguely articulated performance issues, although they seemed focused on work areas and individuals rather than on sweeping organizational concerns/failures. I was, fortunately, called in to advise about recruiting for the trainer position and was able to help management reframe this as "solving for performance needs."

The organization had extensive performance evaluation data, feedback from the public, and success/fail records for professional-level staff. Work performed by paraprofessionals and administrative assistants was largely clerical and easy to review for errors, timeliness, and so forth. Performance issues were dealt with primarily in a reactive fashion. Data was not being leveraged.

### Data
- Past and current performance issues with paraprofessionals and administrative assistants were split between

technical (software/word processing) and interpersonal, with most problems falling on the interpersonal side.

- Data revealed issues with hiring and on-boarding, with performance problems typically occurring in the same work areas most frequently among employees who had been with the agency for less than eighteen months. There were several horror stories about disastrous new hires; documentation from the hiring events showed inadequately defined job descriptions, weak interview questions/procedures, and failure to follow established protocols for panel interviews.

- Issues in particular work areas. No surprise: everyone knew who the weaker managers were. Data showed that it was managers, not workers, who needed help and performance support.

- There was substantive evidence of successes: managers doing well, experienced staff with good performance records, multiple areas with low turnover, and few instances of huge lawsuits or employee complaints.

- Some managers had few opportunities to practice skills like hiring and implementing disciplinary action so the likelihood of error was higher. Others had larger work units/longer history/more experience.

- There were limited funds, partly due to the expectation of hiring a "trainer" at about $50,000 per year.

### Strategy/Solution

Nothing indicated a need for extensive formal training. Compliance requirements, policy and rules overviews, and performance support for software tasks, such as working with word processing or spreadsheet tools, could be delivered via quick online tutorials. Work tasks could be further supported by job aids. The HR benefits officer would continue to provide basic induction activities (signup for health insurance, etc.) on a regular schedule.

Data showed that new managers needed support and that every manager needed support with infrequently performed tasks (some managers of small units had a hiring event only once every few years).

*Strategy:* Use existing talent to support newer staff, those inexperienced with tasks, or those having trouble.

**Solutions**

- *A mentoring program:* The role of mentor was treated as an honor rather than an obligation. Those wishing to become mentors had to apply, stating their qualifications and what they felt they could give in the way of help. Mentors would be named with associated areas of expertise, such as a remarkably strong track record for hiring, a gift for empathy or supervision, or an ability to manage conflict. New managers were matched with a mentor for their first ninety days, at which time they would jointly decide whether to continue. Mentors would receive formal and frequent recognition. A similar program was established for administrative staff. The HR director agreed to serve as manager of the mentoring program to

  - Assign new staff appropriately;

  - Assist when mentoring issues crossed over into HR/ Legal areas; and

- Ensure that mentors were not being unduly burdened with too many mentees: there was legitimate concern that some might become "professional experts" at the expense of their own work.

- *An online "yellow pages"*: Managers enacting infrequently handled tasks were provided with "yellow pages" from which to locate a mentor with given expertise. Individuals volunteered to serve in "expert pools." For instance, hiring managers with the least turnover and biggest success rates volunteered to serve as hiring advisors and were placed in a pool to take turns helping with/serving on hiring panels.

## Results

The solution was built for sustainability: The mentor pool is updated every January. The yellow pages are updated, at minimum, every January. (Increasing comfort levels with social tools seems to have supported the idea of updating the yellow page profiles.) Mentors receive a day of training on basic tasks and purpose—led by an external training consultant and a mentor—and are provided with coaching tools and other support aids. Most mentors have volunteered across several years. Data shows reduced turnover in problem areas and reduced complaints from the public or through the HR office. There have been fewer nightmarish new hire situations, indicating improvement in hiring processes. Most importantly, the perception that every problem can be solved by "training" has changed. Use of the mentors and expert pools, along with performance support tools for technical tasks, offers more rapid resolution and has proven more cost-effective in the short term and more valuable in the long term.

## ALLISON ANDERSON

I first heard of Allison through Jay Cross and, subsequently, was impressed with her focus on finding out what people needed, so much so that I interviewed her for an article for *Chief Learning Officer* magazine. In her quiet way, she continues to advocate for a human-centered approach to supporting learning. She graciously provided this case study baring real issues from her work when she was with Intel.

### What Are the Organization's Characteristics?

L&D at Intel is very decentralized. At last count, there are over fifty organizations developing and/or delivering learning solutions to our 100K+ employee base. More than 350 people are within those orgs—and they range from a single person developing PowerPoint to a centralized HR L&D group of about fifty providing a full soft skills curriculum to employees, managers, and leaders within the company (in other words, to all 100K employees).

While this model helps us provide learning as close to the need as possible, it has created some inefficiencies due to a lack of communication between groups. Learning practitioners often worked in isolation—particularly those in the very small groups. Innovation in this type of environment is extremely slow and difficult to achieve. We haven't been able to create a seamless experience for our employees, for example. There are multiple LMSs, departmental websites serving as learning portals, and so on. It is a pretty fractured environment.

### What Situation Did You Come Into?

Back in 1999, we had even more organizations and more people developing training (as opposed to learning) for the masses. Multiple groups were starting to dip their toes into the world of elearning, but no one knew what tools to use or what good design looked like. People were operating in the dark, each org and each person trying to solve problems on its own. Very inefficient, and frustrating for all concerned. It really started jeopardizing whether we could move forward and innovate.

A couple of people from different departments happened to connect and discovered that they were all trying to solve the same problems and find the right tools. So they decided to get together and share best-known methods (BKMs) with each other. That was the germ the led to the creation of the Technology Based Training (TBT) Task Force.

I came in a couple of years later, to a group of about thirty. Over the years I've built the membership in many ways, but we've never done a real marketing campaign. Most folks come in through word of mouth or when we reach out to folks regarding special events. From that handful of people, we've now evolved into the Learning Community of Practice (LCoP), a group of more than 350 L&D practitioners from across the business groups at Intel.

## What Was Your Strategic Plan?

Our plan, really, is to share knowledge and expertise. We do this in lots of ways:

- Monthly meetings where members share their current or completed projects, current issues, or corporate updates (like changes to our LMS) and where we discuss what's on the horizon—industry trends, the future of learning, et cetera;

- Special events where we bring in external speakers;

- A knowledge sharing site (SharePoint) where we post meeting materials and case studies. We've just launched a contest for sharing short demo videos, a la Khan Academy. So we look for many different ways that we can gather and share our expertise;

- A community on our social computing platform (Planet Blue), where we have discussions, post job openings, ask burning questions, and where I and my co-lead blog occasionally (but not enough).

- Multi-day events, occasionally, where we gather for a professional development conference. We aren't funded to do this annually, but we look for ways we can gather virtually in a highly engaging way in order to create deeper connections and have more in-depth learning opportunities. I'm sure this is true in other organizations—our L&D people rarely have the opportunity to attend conferences. Our gatherings are often the closest they come to professional development. So we take this very seriously and really strive to do what we can with no budget—although we love to meet in-person. We improvise and do as much as we can, trying to be as creative as possible in our opportunities.

**How Is It Working?**

It works very well, as long as we remember who we are and why we are together. A few times over the past we've tried to over-reach. The membership includes people at different levels in the organization, and sometimes we think we can drive change that is really beyond our control. Recently, Intel has formed the Intel Learning Leadership Network, which brings together senior learning leaders from across the company. The

LCoP serves as a knowledge network and also a great place to obtain feedback on corporate initiatives. We can influence to a large extent, and we are certainly the group that implements change. But the decision body rests a level or two higher in most cases, and that's where the ILLN comes in.

As long as we have a clear mission and objectives, we do great. When we over-reach, we are not as successful.

We have good participation—a core group of fifty to seventy people rotate in and out of active attendance. That's a good size, as far as I'm concerned. The information flow in the wider network is good, but could always improve. We are still building the repository of knowledge, and we continue to play with the best way to deliver community information and encourage participation.

## What Advice Would You Give to Others?

Well, funny you should ask. I have given a number of presentations about the LCoP, and I've honed in on what I think are the areas that make us successful and what I think can help other groups like ours be successful. Here are the key points:

- *Purpose and identity:* Be very clear about the purpose of the cross-functional group. Always lead with "why." Why are you together? What do you hope to accomplish? This should be promoted and posted in as many places as possible, so that the group and new members have clear expectations. Similarly, have a very clear identity. By that I mean the little things—like we have met the third Thursday of the month since our inception over ten years ago. Even when I try to suggest changing it, folks tell me they like it because they know they can count on it. Also—and this may be totally dumb but who cares—my highly entertaining dog has become an unofficial mascot for us. He's made appearances during our events via webcam (the first time, he was a puppy chewing and destroying all of the electronics in the room—he left an impression), or I'll post a photo of him in some adventure. Whatever it is, it kind of gives us some personality.

- *Engagement and content:* You need to look for creative ways to encourage participation. If you are in a synchronous meeting, throw up a whiteboard and have everyone type in their answers to a question regarding the topic. Or create discussion groups that build on your blog entries. Run a competition on content creation. Try many things and see what sticks. But be aware that you need to be adding value, so be sure you have some content to offer. Here again, the engagement is important. You want to share that responsibility and gather the tribal wisdom. Of course, you may be running a different type of group and maybe you have designated experts and don't have broad group participation. Whatever your model, you need content.

- *Leadership and support:* First of all, in many situations you would do well to find a good sponsor in a fairly senior position. Second, it is my experience that you really do want a leader for your community; things just don't happen organically. There's a lot going on in anyone's workday, and if everything is left to the general membership at large, you can get stalled. I think this quote says it well: "While the power is in the hands of the community members, having a thoughtful guide, beacon, and evangelist is the key lynchpin role in building and maintaining a successful online presence." (from Community Roundtable 2010 State of Community Management Report)

- *Tools and processes:* Think through the tools you use within the community and, as with any learning solution, use the best tool for the task. One thing I like about the LCoP in particular is that we can be a kind of microcosm of the Intel learning experience. By that I mean that we can try out new tools ourselves and actually experience them before we integrate them into our departmental offerings. Anyway, we used to do everything by email, and then we started using SharePoint, and then, after our Social Computing platform launched, we were early adopters and transferred most of our communication over there. But we found over time that Planet Blue wasn't a good fit for everything and we've started to rotate back to SharePoint for much of the knowledge repository.

- *Impact and results:* Impact is so important, and so hard to prove. It's very hard to collect quantitative data about the impact of the community. We track some numbers as far as membership and participation, but we know that's not a good yardstick for impact. So we'll try to gather qualitative input—What is the perceived value of the community, how has it improved your workflow or your experience as a learning practitioner at Intel? We try to set up success criteria for small projects (like our SharePoint update or our conference project team) and report on those data points.

## CHARLES JENNINGS

I had the pleasure of getting to know Charles when Jay Cross pulled us together through the Internet Time Alliance, which has been a personal boon owing to his wisdom and personability. Charles had been the chief learning officer at Reuters after a long career integrating business, learning, and technology.

He's currently director of the 70:20:10 Forum and Duntroon Associates, as well as a member of the Internet Time Alliance. He has provided this exemplary story of his approach at Reuters.

### What Were the Organization's Characteristics?

When I joined the Reuters organization in late 2001, it was with the remit to "transform training" across the organization and build a truly coherent, global learning function. In 2001 Reuters was a 150-year-old company with a proud history as the world's leading independent news and information provider. The company values were encapsulated in its credo of "speed, accuracy, and freedom from bias."

Reuters had grown solidly from its beginnings in London in 1851, when the young German émigré Paul Julius Reuter moved the two-year-old prototype news service he had established in Aachen, for which he used the emerging technology of electric telegraphy together with the tested technology of carrier pigeons.

In 2001 the culture of Reuters was one that held its history as being important, but one that was also looking to create innovative solutions for its clients, news organizations and financial institutions around the world. The Reuters Group comprised nearly eighteen thousand people working in ninety-four countries worldwide. The company was producing some eight million words every day in more than twenty-six languages, as well as a constant stream of financial data that was updated some twenty-three thousand times per second at peak trading times.

## What Situation Did You Come Into?

Despite its significant global footprint and brand, Reuters operated to a large extent as if it were a set of discrete independent companies. This was understandable to an extent because, at the time, the group consisted of more than one hundred distinct legal entities.

This was reflected within the training function. Each continent had its regional training manager and team, with other teams scattered through the various functional business units. If the case could be argued to senior business unit leaders, then very often a budget was found to set up a new training team. There was no central coordination or oversight and no common standards or resource sharing.

On examination, training budgets were being 200 percent overspent (there were no central checks in place) and in the previous eighteen months more than three thousand providers of training and learning-related services had been used—one for every six employees! There were no vendor management processes or systems in place, and no strategy to adopt 21st Century learning approaches.

## What Was Your Strategic Plan?

Put simply, the plan I presented to the senior leadership consisted of a single strategic initiative—to move from what was exclusive event-based training provision to a process-based learning service.

"From event to process" became my catch-cry.

Of course, alongside the high-level vision, we also set about the practical work of understanding the cost base in detail, including where and how budget was being allocated and spent, and identifying or creating processes that were both global in nature and execution and reflected a learning service that was focused on generating organizational and business impact in an efficient and effective manner.

We mapped our challenge in this way (see Figure 8.1).

The focus initially was on creating efficiencies by removing duplication of effort and cost and on establishing standards that could be applied globally. My view was (and still is) that the "twin pillars" of standards (technical standards and quality standards) and infrastructure (human and technical) form a critical platform for establishing a robust and fit-for-purpose learning & development operation.

A 70:20:10 strategy sat over the entire plan. It was clear that the focus on structured learning alone (and most of it through face-to-face classroom and workshop delivery) was ignoring the huge potential benefits that workplace and social learning offered. The 70:20:10 model offered a much better base to build an effective learning and performance strategy.

## How Did It Work?

Over a period of four years, Reuters grew its internal learning services from an essentially classroom-based training model to a much richer environment with both "push" and "pull" services.

In the 70:20:10-enabled service, employees could attend workshops and courses when needed or access elearning or blended services if they suited better. They had access to online materials and support. Coaching and mentoring was strengthened across the company and, importantly, technology was

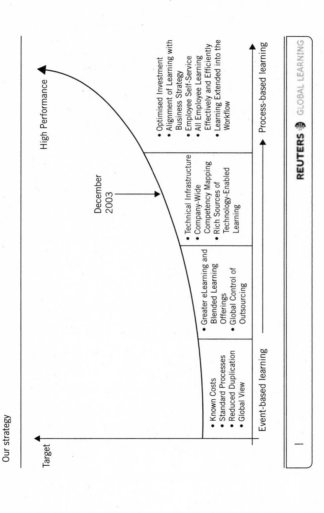

Our strategy

Target

High Performance

December 2003

- Optimised Investment
- Alignment of Learning with Business Strategy
- Employee Self-Service
- All Employee Learning Effectively and Efficiently
- Learning Extended into the Workflow

- Technical Infrastructure
- Company-Wide Competency Mapping
- Rich Sources of Technology-Enabled Learning

- Greater eLearning and Blended Learning Offerings
- Global Control of Outsourcing

- Known Costs
- Standard Processes
- Reduced Duplication
- Global View

Event-based learning

Process-based learning

REUTERS 🌐 GLOBAL LEARNING

**Figure 8.1** Strategy Map

deployed in many forms—from introducing a standard, global, learning management platform (previously, we had identified eight LMSs and fifteen training administration systems in use), to deploying an electronic performance support system (EPSS) and various social learning environments.

Exclusive virtual provision was also deployed. The Reuters Institute of Technology was rolled out to support technical employees across the world. The Institute offered no physical courses, but a wealth of resources and communities of interest, as well as links with external experts and online testing tools for technical employees to check their capabilities and map individual learning paths.

The 70:20:10 strategy had significant impact for the company across the globe. The words of Tom Glocer, the CEO of Reuters and Thomson Reuters, probably best describe the impact achieved by the entire learning and development team:

---

"You have made real lasting contributions to Reuters and now Thomson Reuters. You took us from only face-to-face learning into a modern era we claim to provide to our customers."

Thomas Glocer, CEO Thomson<br>Reuters, 23 December 2008.

---

## What Advice Would You Give to Others?

The implementation of any strategy takes time, and it usually takes longer than planned. No matter how many resources are allocated to managing the processes, or how large your project office is, it is almost a rule of life that things take longer than expected. To deliver effective transformation it is necessary to plan a clear vision and path, but to be adaptable and flexible in its execution. Often, technologies will change under your feet, organizational structures and priorities also. You need to be adaptable and to continually look for the "low-hanging fruit"—the areas and actions that will reap rewards quickly and easily.

It is also vital that you continually develop your skills and capabilities and that of your teams and embrace a culture of self-development and collaborative development. Only those organizations that nurture sharing and networking, where employees can openly ask questions and share their expertise with colleagues, will thrive. Those stuck in a time warp of structured "knowledge transfer" and the belief that each person is an island will lose out.

Only those people and organizations that can embrace a culture of innovation and controlled risk taking will succeed. Technology is critical. Without technology you will forever be trapped in the "richness-reach tradeoff"—trying, and usually failing, to support dispersed workforces with rich development opportunities.

## ASSESS YOURSELF

At this point, it becomes sensible to assess where you are relative to where you could, and should, be. Across such a wide variety of areas, however, there's no one obvious instrument to use. Candidates would include Research Dog's eLearning Readiness Assessment (Chapnick, 2001), although it is specific to elearning. The eLearning Maturity Model from Toward Maturity (Overton & Dixon, 2013) is another candidate, again specific to technology, however. The Community

Maturity Model from The Community Roundtable (2009) is robust specifically around social learning, but does not cover the complete spectrum. On the flip side, the Human Capital Capability Scorecard (Bassi, McGraw, and McMurrer, 2004) is much broader, but actually goes beyond the scope of what is being focused on here.

As a consequence of the dearth of possibilities, presented here is an ad hoc assessment based on the performance ecosystem model elements with a principled attempt to create a top-level assessment in each of the areas, adding in the areas of metrics and culture to broaden from technology to L&D as a whole (see Table 8.1). The goal is to determine what would constitute stages for each of the component areas. The four steps are

- Unaware of the opportunities,
- Initiating movement,
- At a mature stage, and
- At the leading edge.

We start by breaking the framework of culture into two dimensions: the culture about learning and the orientation of the overall mission of the organization (see Table 8.2). Within the learning culture, a competitive approach is ultimately destructive. If it's not safe to share, you can't learn together. A cooperative culture is a step up, where people will help one another when asked. An improvement on that is when folks naturally pitch in together to help one another meet the organizational needs. Ideally, individuals will work together to improve each other and themselves, as well as the organization.

**Table 8.1** L&D Assessment

| Category | Component | Unaware | Initiating | Mature | Leading |
|---|---|---|---|---|---|
| Culture | Learning | Competitive | Cooperative | Collaborative | Continual Improvement |
| | Orientation | Self | Community | Organization | Society |
| Formal | Design | Knowledge Focus | Engaging/Lean | Meaningful | Experience |
| | Use | Service Model | Mixed | Aligned | Discerning |
| Performance Focus | Aids | By Operating Unit | Created | Curated | Shared |
| Social | Portal | Siloed | Idiosyncratic | User-Centered | Dynamic |
| | Network | External | Idiosyncratic | Supported | Empowered |
| | Usage | Resistant | Hesitant | Confident | Engaged |
| Infrastructure | Content Model | Implicit | Chunked | Designed | Adaptive |
| | Semantics | None | Default | Designed | Emergent |
| Metrics | Summative | Efficiency | Effectiveness | Informal | Entrenched |
| | Formative | Users | Customers | Outcomes | Balanced |

**Table 8.2** Culture Assessment

| Category | Component | Unaware | Initiating | Mature | Leading |
|---|---|---|---|---|---|
| Culture | Learning | Competitive | Cooperative | Collaborative | Continual Improvement |
| | Orientation | Self | Community | Organization | Society |

**Table 8.3** Formal Learning Assessment

| Category | Component | Unaware | Initiating | Mature | Leading |
|---|---|---|---|---|---|
| Formal | Design | Knowledge Focus | Engaging/Lean | Meaningful | Experience |
| | Use | Service Model | Mixed | Aligned | Discerning |

The orientation of the L&D organization itself impacts its overall success. By focusing beyond the individual to the community (and work teams), organizations start tapping into the power of people. By spreading that across the organization, the benefits learned from one area can be spread to others, raising the game. By contributing back to the society, as manifested through the network, the organization becomes part of a larger ecosystem and creates a broader and more beneficial reputation.

Formal learning is a second area (see Table 8.3). Formal can be broken into the way in which the learning team focused on design and the way that formal learning is used within the organization. On the design side, without being aware it is easy for a learning organization to take the information from the SME and focus on knowledge, a step up is to add in the emotional component as well as stripping away unnecessary padding. The real step up is to focus on making the learning meaningful in several ways: it's aligned with the organizational need and tested against organizational outcomes, as well as made directly relevant to the learners. Finally, the ideal is to go beyond the learning event and recognize the need for learning experiences with sufficient depth and breadth, distributed across media and contexts.

The second factor is how the unit as a whole is responding to perceived need. Too often, organizations "take orders" for learning and develop as requested. A more astute focus is to look across needs and, while meeting needs, begin to look for opportunities to add real strategic value. Ensuring that all investments are aligned with real business needs and not doing learning when it isn't impacting key metrics is a step up. Ultimately, the organization can and should be prioritizing investment effort solely on the unique opportunities that formal learning can be providing and using the full suite of solutions as well as the formal ones.

When shifting to consider a performance focus (see Table 8.4), there are two elements: supporting by putting information in the world and making the support accessible in ways that make sense to the performer. To address the aids themselves, currently such support can be provided by each business unit, with no coherent strategy. A more enlightened approach is to process these through a unit that can add knowledge of how work is done and how information is processed. The next stage is to not create all that are necessary, but curating across resources developed internally and externally, only creating when necessary. Ultimately, a shared responsibility for development and curation will be shared between L&D and the communities themselves.

As a second stage, we need to also consider how access to these support resources is enabled. Beyond having resources siloed by business unit, initial efforts to have them aligned by task is a start. A more comprehensive approach is to have a user-centric focus; by user role and community makes sense. Ultimately, dynamic resource availability considering user, context, and task will be the way to go.

When it comes to social (see Table 8.5), we again have two elements: how the organization is leveraging the network and individual attitudes toward using the network. In the former case, many companies constrain social access, not recognizing that now—with mobile devices—there is no way to block the signal. Some access may be allowed or some groups may use software, but really supporting the use of social software or providing a rich suite is a step ahead. Providing support to

**Table 8.4** Performance Focus

| Category | Component | Unaware | Initiating | Mature | Leading |
|---|---|---|---|---|---|
| Performance Focus | Aids | By Operating Unit | Created | Curated | Shared |
|  | Portal | Siloed | Idiosyncratic | User-Centered | Dynamic |

**Table 8.5** Social Learning Assessment

| Category | Component | Unaware | Initiating | Mature | Leading |
|---|---|---|---|---|---|
| Social | Network | External | Idiosyncratic | Supported | Empowered |
|  | Usage | Resistant | Hesitant | Confident | Engaged |

empower people to leverage the network by developing skills is at the cutting edge.

The way such environments are used, too, is critical. For a variety of reasons, users may be resistant. With some support they can be hesitant but willing. With both emotional and skill support, users can be confident. When individuals are constructively taking ownership and developing value for each other, the network is fully engaged.

Moving beyond the interventions, there are levels to developing the infrastructure as well (see Table 8.6). Note that the integration of systems at the back end is assumed, as no one system is currently, or likely ever should be, able to deliver all the necessary capability. Similarly, flexible delivery across devices is assumed as an outflow of an integrated system. As a consequence, the two levels include focusing on structure around the content and the additional information to support systematic leverage. For the content model, the lack of one is the typical approach. A more structured approach is to chunk the content more granularly. A major improvement is to design models for content to be developed into. Finally, having sufficient structure around the content to support flexible use, adapting to different learners, contexts, tasks, and more, is a desirable possibility.

The second necessary level for infrastructure is the semantics attached to the content (and the rules that leverage the associated semantic labeling). Of course, little is typically done, but default labels can be leveraged. A second level is for an organization to systematically design and leverage a suite of tags and associated rules. Ultimately, an organization should also systematically track and leverage emergent rules as well.

The metrics we use to evaluate what we are doing have to change as well (see Table 8.7). Two different areas here include

**Table 8.6** Infrastructure Assessment

| Category | Component | Unaware | Initiating | Mature | Leading |
|---|---|---|---|---|---|
| Infrastructure | Content Model | *Implicit* | *Chunked* | *Designed* | *Adaptive* |
| | Semantics | *None* | *Default* | *Designed* | *Emergent* |

**Table 8.7** Metrics Assessment

| Category | Component | Unaware | Initiating | Mature | Leading |
|---|---|---|---|---|---|
| Metrics | Summative | *Efficiency* | *Effectiveness* | *Informal* | *Entrenched* |
| | Formative | *Users* | *Customers* | *Outcomes* | *Balanced* |

how we evaluate the impact of what we do and how we evaluate what we're doing to determine whether it's "cooked." For the former, as discussed earlier, efficiency is a measure we often use, but it's not of much interest unless we are also being effective. Going further, we should be measuring informal learning as well. Finally, having evaluation baked into everything we do is the way we should be moving.

We should also be upgrading our formative evaluation. Asking the learners is, by itself, not particularly effective, since they don't necessarily know what they really need. Looking for the impact on customers is an improvement, but as Steve Jobs is quoted as saying: "People don't know what they want until you show it to them" (*Business Week Online*, 1998). Of course, seeing how initial versions impact in experiments and tuning until you find the outcomes you intend to achieve is the real goal. Finally, balancing to achieve customer satisfaction and employee preference as well as business impact is the ultimate triangulation for the improvement you want to achieve.

With an awareness of where you are, you are prepared to determine where you want to be, where to start, and how to get there.

## BOTTOM LINE

The role of L&D is different:

- Employees will feel a much tighter alignment between organizational performance and L&D interventions.
- Much more awareness of corporate culture will be felt throughout the organization.

- The focus of managers and executives will shift to leadership and support, rather than managing.

- L&D's role will shift to facilitation and curation, with a much diminished role of creation and presentation.

So what does it take to get there?

# 9

# Re-Think

Even with a clear vision of where you want to be, it's not clear how you can get there. While what follows is not a definitive guide, it does capture the best emergent thinking in the space. The path forward is to have a starting point, some clear guidelines, and then experiment and refine. Practicing what we preach, you should join or create a work team composed of members of different communities who can contribute to the development of your approach, as well as provide a mechanism for new insights to be integrated and outcomes to be shared. The starting point needs to be a strategy that refocuses efforts to align with the new understanding of how we learn and how we work alone and together.

Donald H. Taylor, chairman of the Learning and Performance Institute, has aptly unpacked the problem in terms of two dimensions: the pace at which the organization is adapting and the rate at which L&D is adapting (see Figure 9.1). If organizations are not adapting quickly, it is okay that L&D is not, and they can both head comfortably toward extinction.

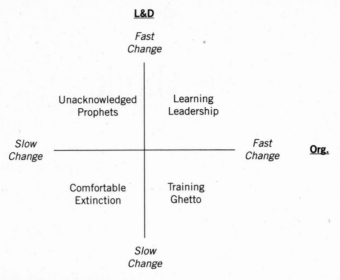

**Figure 9.1** The Training Ghetto
Adapted from Donald H. Taylor © 2013, by permission.

If L&D is adapting quickly, but the organization is not, the L&D leadership are unacknowledged prophets. If L&D is adapting at the rate of change of the organization, L&D is demonstrating learning leadership. However, the evidence is increasingly that L&D is, largely, in the "training ghetto," not adapting at the rate the organization requires.

The clear need, then, is for L&D to rethink and realign to become an agile partner in organizational changes.

## PERFORMANCE AS STRATEGY

The real shift has to be from training, or learning, to performance. The *outcome* is what matters. How you get there is secondary. Whether the answer comes from performance support or via the network, if it solves the problem it is every bit as valid as if it comes from training.

If you look at the two components to success, optimal execution and continual innovation, you will see a wide variety of elements that can contribute to this success (see Figure 9.2). Traditionally, training to support optimal execution, and perhaps performance support, have been covered. Indeed, many organizations have formal mentoring and coaching solutions, as well, and some education options. Cooperation and collaboration, however, have largely been individual responsibilities, as has personal knowledge management (PKM). Integrating these into a coherent whole, in a way that is focused on both assisting individuals to perform in the moment and developing them over time, must be the new focus. In that sense, training or L&D is no longer sufficient. Really, a more apt description is performance and development, or P&D.

The overarching function, then, shows the core roles in P&D to be performance consulting on the side of optimizing execution and facilitation on the side of continual innovation. There are associated skills, to be certain, including learning experience and resource design, information architecture, conversation facilitation, curation, and more. The essential idea, however, has to be focused on ensuring that the core tasks are done at a high level and that the ongoing development of the organization's intellectual capital and the individuals who generate that value is proceeding with a rich awareness of how people learn and work.

This is not just strategic; it is also pragmatic. With the increasing rate of competition and consequent information

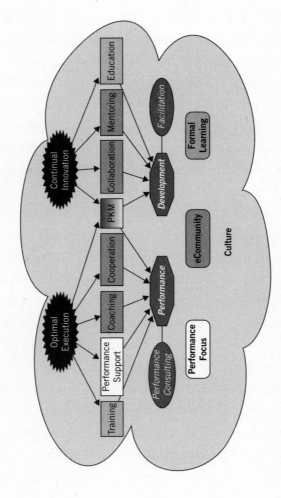

**Figure 9.2** Performance & Development

churn, with the increasing suite of software tools being used and their complexity, and with the more flexible shifts in business unit strategy, the information need is growing and changing faster than training can address it. Most organizations are finding that they cannot continue to meet the demand and therefore must find ways to address the need with new techniques.

## DOING LESS

In addition to the focus on performance, a concomitant value that both improves the individual experience and makes the P&D group more effective is a focus on doing *the least possible*. This manifests in several ways.

The most obvious way is to be leaner in our design. Our performance support should be weaned to the bare minimum, and our formal designs should be trimmed down and focus only on meaningful behavior. No "nice to have" should be tolerated.

A second way is to, as much as possible, find the answer elsewhere. This starts by seeing whether the answer can come from the network. If it's out there, let the network handle it. This is good not just for minimizing effort, but for building bonds in the network itself.

Another way to look for answers elsewhere is to curate resources. While the network will do some of this, P&D can and should, too. Facilitation then means modeling the behaviors that the community will have to take over, including curation.

It also means not making a course to meet every request. A minimalist focus means focusing only on those things that are unique to the organization and directing the needy else-where. Don't develop anything unless you have to and you know what the business benefit is.

Our focus has to be on doing the most good with the fewest resources. This may seem obvious, but with a broader repertoire come decisions about the best place to allocate effort and expenditure.

## LEARNING AS CULTURE

You may have the best plans and intentions, but if there's a mismatch with the culture, those plans are for naught. The core point is to create an environment in which learning transformation can happen. This includes addressing the tra-ditional organizational change components, along with culture change.

How do you change culture? This is not an insignificant issue, and quite simply, culture is the biggest barrier to change. While this is not the place to address the full process, some quick guidance indicates that you can't just decree it. Culture is a collected set of behaviors and values that have developed over time and define an organization. Behaviors manifest as hab-its, and values as attitudes. Changing either of those requires top-level buy-in, selling a new vision (perhaps making the problems concrete), looking for leverage points, and support-ing the change by rewarding new behaviors, celebrating the benefits of change, and reinforcing the values.

Peter de Jager, in *Pocketful of Change* (2011), suggests that individuals need to feel that they have chosen the change. His recommendations included: (1) sell them on the why, then support the how; (2) help them know what will not change and what they need to do differently; and (3) have a plan for when things go wrong.

What new culture do you want? As discussed earlier, the major elements of a successful culture that supports a learning environment include a safe place to contribute, openness to and appreciation for new ideas, and time for reflection. Leadership that not only supports but models the process helps. And being explicit about the value and means for learning is necessary as well.

The benefits are many. When you are open to new ideas that come from diversity, because it is safe to share and people have time to reflect, you have an opportunity for innovation. When people understand the value of learning, they are empowered to take control of their own learning and open to the available resources.

There are, of course, many ways to go wrong and some difficult issues. It has to be safe to fail, and yet you do not want to celebrate failure nor make avoidable mistakes. A lovely story I heard at a small company was that they rang a bell, not when the mistake was made, but when the lesson was learned. That powerful difference made it okay to fail, but also helped to prevent anyone else from making the same mistake.

If it's not safe to fail, if "anything you say can and will be held against you," however, people won't contribute. If the culture is so competitive that anyone who admits a mistake will be ostracized or someone else will use it as leverage to climb the ladder, learning won't happen. Companies that can't admit mistakes are doomed to repeat them.

The alternative is to share your work and learn out loud. By sharing, everyone gets ahead faster and better. Sharing has to be valued. When you put in a social media system and no one contributes, there's a problem. It may be culture, it may be design, but if it is not working, you are missing out on the opportunity to leverage collective intelligence.

I believe the two key words are "trust" and "transparency." Trust that workers will give their best to achieve the objectives, and trust that the leaders are focusing on meaningful goals. That trust is facilitated by transparency, showing not only the results, but also the underlying thinking and intermediate results. Similarly, one must trust that the transparency will be used to further the outcomes of the organization.

You cannot fake it. Your employees will react to the real culture, not the touted culture. If the real culture is not aligned with the purported culture, you not only miss the opportunity to benefit, but you undermine employee loyalty.

The culture change has to be fundamental. You cannot bolt new culture on top of the old. Culture just is. Whatever your employees believe about the benefits of contributing cannot be dealt with unless you address what those same employees believe about what the company values.

This does not mean that you must wait until the culture has changed to begin working on strategy. Nor does it mean that if you do not (yet) have such a culture, you have no reason to change. There are benefits to the strategic changes, even if you cannot leverage all the opportunity that comes from continual innovation. On the other hand, you have to create a culture in which the refocus on performance can happen. And that refocus will affect the culture as well. Culture and strategy change are inextricably linked. The benefits of a richer approach to optimal execution are an argument all in itself, but the richer picture is found in integrating strategy and culture.

## ORGANIZATION

This strategy suggests some structural changes in the organization. For one, Performance & Development should ultimately be at the same executive level as IT (and tightly coupled to it), and just as ubiquitous across the enterprise. There will be different roles, although existing staff can likely and desirably be migrated into these new positions. Different measurements should also be used, and there may be reorganization to align more closely with business needs.

The role changes imply that there will most likely be facilitators within different business units and that performance consultants may be distributed or rotate to assignments as needed. The structure of the P&D unit may change as well. There may be a core team providing design support for performance support and elearning (media and learning design), virtual classroom and face-to-face facilitation, as well as some other roles.

There will be changes in the metrics that are used to evaluate the impact of the P&D unit and changes in the metrics that P&D uses to evaluate their own efforts. The performance impact and the facilitation impact will have to be seen, and the effectiveness of those initiatives will also be evaluated. Ultimately, efficiency will come into play, but only after impact.

The required skills will shift. The Learning and Performance Institute uses a Capability Map to assess individual capability (2013). This instrument documents the necessary skills required for an enlightened approach to L&D, with twenty-seven skills across nine categories (see Appendix A). ASTD has developed a Competency Model across ten categories of meaningful skills and six foundational competencies (see Appendix C; Arneson, Rothwell, & Naughton, 2013). The goal, however, is not to replace people with others possessing these skills, but instead to develop these skills in people already possessing some subset of them. It also is likely that, in most cases, different people will have different roles, so some may be performance consultants while others could be development facilitators.

## SUPPORTING WORK

Another way to think about the role of P&D is not about learning, but as supporting work. If the work is learning, and learning is the work, then supporting work is supporting learning.

The way of looking at action in the world described in Chapter 4 (see Figure 4.1) suggests that the role of P&D is supporting the different tasks when we do not know the answers (see Figure 9.3). Roles for support are present at each stage. On the performance side, we should be ensuring that there are directories of expertise and skills to help identify those with the answer or viable and useful collaborators with diverse and complementary skills. We should be creating and curating resources to support performance and providing tools to capture new solutions, processes, and aids.

On the facilitation side, many skills can be developed, and these should not be assumed. The ability to search and

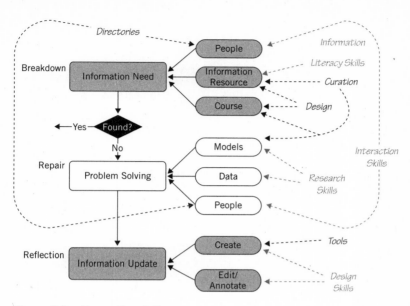

**Figure 9.3**   Supporting Action

find resources, for instance, cannot be taken for granted. Similarly, the ability to interact with others to ask for help and work together is an area for facilitation that some may not possess. Research skills and the ability to systematically use data and analytics to answer questions, as well as to acquire and interpret relevant research, are areas that must be supported. Finally, the ability to design resources that support performance and capture new learning can be facilitated as well.

By looking at how we work, we can think anew about how we can support work. With a performance and development perspective, new opportunities and a new alignment with the organization become visible.

**BOTTOM LINE**

Some changes are both necessary and desirable:

- The culture has to be supportive of learning.
- The strategy has to focus on the dual goals of optimal performance and continual innovation.
- Optimal performance must be supported by design.
- Continual innovation has to be supported by facilitation.

From this point, we need to redesign what we do.

# Leader Reflections

When I think of the pioneers who were articulating the need to go beyond courses long before others caught on, two names immediately spring to mind. I thought it appropriate to have them bridge the gap between principle and practice, as they have played that role for the industry.

Both are articulate writers and engaging speakers, and have a keen ability to cut through the hype and get to the heart of an issue. They have served as role models through their work with societies such as the International Society for Performance Improvement (ISPI) and the American Society for Training and Development (ASTD). In addition to numerous other awards, both are eLearning Guild "Guild Masters."

I asked them to share their thoughts on some of the key questions we face. They were kind enough to agree, and I have the great honor here to introduce Drs. Allison Rossett and Marc Rosenberg and share their reflections.

## ALLISON ROSSETT

Allison, now professor emeritus at San Diego State University and consulting through allisonrossett.com, is a long-term example of clear thinking around organizational learning. She has been a strong advocate of looking at and doing the research, not just following the trends. The author of a number of books that have helped shape practices in the industry, she has written on using technology in workplace learning, practical task analysis, performance support, and more. Her witty and practical advice is well worth listening to.

## What Do You See as the Needed Change in L&D?

*The* needed change? Only one? Well, I guess if I had to pick one it would be to move workplace learning professionals into the field, in an attempt to rivet their attention to the challenges and cultures of the organization.

The most compelling complaint I hear about L&D people is that we aren't realistic enough, aren't sufficiently practical about what is top of mind in the field. Clustering at headquarters does not lend itself to focus on the field and on the work, workers, and workplace.

## What Are Organizations Doing Well?

Of course, it varies. I know some that are doing some nifty things with mobile devices, others who are squeezing value from their LMSs, still others who are getting the leader/manager thing done well through a combination of development and support.

Let me share an example of some wonderfulness I encountered in a financial services institution. They were bringing several organizations together across many miles and even from different countries. Each entity had its own ways of doing people development and support, of course. One of their strategies, among many, was to develop their instructional designers along parallel lines, setting shared expectations and helping them move in those directions. While commencing with expectations, it also involved training, examples, supervision, accountability, and teamed projects across boundaries. Another aspect, one I was involved with in particular, was to create an online home and hub to encourage continuous dialogue.

## What Are Organizations Still Messing Up?

I guess that is what I was describing above. It just isn't good enough to read *our* journals and books and blogs, although I advocate it, of course. Workplace learning professionals must read what their customers and clients read. How else will they know what keeps them up at night?

Other mess-ups:

- Adoration for shiny pennies

- Many plans, less execution

- Failure to ask hard questions, gather data, examine the data already extant in the organization

- Failure to tend to relationships with line leaders and managers

- Difficulties attracting the best and brightest experts and thought leaders to the table to contribute to the "stuff" of people and organization development

## How Can Organizations Go from Where They Are to Where They Need to Be?

It depends. Where do they mess up and why? I don't want to be flip about this, but there is no one solution here. What is slowing progress in *your* situation? In some cases, the issue is habits. We do what we do because we have always done it. In other cases, we are doing what we do because something caught the eye of an executive.

If you want to get somewhere, first you have to be clear about where you are going and why it is worthy of commitment. Then you have to ask hard questions about it, questions that ask why, questions that are all about human performance and systems. If we are talking about something new (product, philosophy, technology), we must be anticipatory. What will get in the way? Skills? Knowledge? Motivation? Context? Incentives? What metrics will inspect these selected expectations? Are the players lined up to make a good idea become a reality?

## MARC ROSENBERG

Marc has been one of the early, consistent, and eloquent advocates of a strategic approach to elearning. His landmark book, *Beyond e-Learning* (2006), integrated disparate concepts about using technology "beyond the course" into a coherent whole. Drawing from his years in industry, his regular column at *Learning Solutions* magazine (learningsolutionsmag.com), "Marc My Words," always offers an insightful look at elearning issues. Marc consults through Marc Rosenberg and Associates at www.marcrosenberg.com/.

### What Do You See as the Needed Change in L&D?

On the surface, one can argue that real change in the L&D world is actually happening as a result of the perfect storm of new and cheaper technologies, budget cuts, and mobility/decentralization. That said, I am afraid we could move faster if not for some changes that are harder to implement and accept. I think one of our struggles comes from within the L&D community. I believe that front-line managers and executives are far more willing than training folks to look at performance issues differently. We really need to take a hard look in the mirror. When we do, we'll likely see processes and perceptions that must change, including, but not limited to, the assumption that training cures all ills. Another needed change relates not to the development of new technologies, but to how we use them (for example, social media). They are enablers and not strategies. Having great technology with no strategy may simply allow you to do the wrong things more efficiently. Technology is critical, but too often we start—and stop— there. Finally, another major change for L&D has to do with venues. Classes and training centers are fine for some things, but increasingly, we must become more involved in workplace learning. This is more than elearning . . . it includes performance support, knowledge management, coaching and mentoring, and much more.

## What Are Organizations Doing Well?

I think organizations are getting better at training design and development, although this is not a universal perspective. There are, however, pockets of excellence where organizations are building better instructional materials and better integrating them in the workplace. With mobility a big deal, organizations are moving faster to reach workers any time and anywhere, a good thing. These are the role model organizations; I wish we had better case studies of what they do well. I also think we are more skillful at managing our resources, internal and external. Perhaps the recent budget crises that every organization seems to have been through forced better management of L&D functions. Finally, I think organizations are more open minded about new approaches. This does not mean they will adopt them, but increasingly, many L&D organizations know, deep down, that change is needed. The glass is half-full.

## What Are Organizations Still Messing Up?

I could write pages on this, but succinctly, here goes. . . . Many L&D organizations cling too hard to past practices, claiming "it ain't broke, so why fix it?" The problem is that, when it breaks, it breaks in a big way and there is little time to recover. In the "you can have it good, fast, or cheap—pick two" scenario, many organizations, intentionally or not, give up on the "good." We tend to follow some processes (e.g., ADDIE, instructional objectives, etc.) too blindly. We are always looking for the cheapest way to get something done. The rapid elearning ease may have done more damage than it helped. Even L&D organizations that "get" the changes that need to be made are ill-equipped to sell them to upper management. They are willing to look at what changes are needed, but for many reasons are incapable of pulling the trigger to get it done. The culture of the organization is just too harsh and the organizational expectations are too traditional (because, in part, we've spent forty years setting them). We're weak in evaluation and assessment, business case development, and developing solid value propositions for L&D. We embrace informal learning, knowledge management, performance support, social learning, and so forth, but we have no real idea how to successfully sell or implement these crucial changes. Finally, few organizations are paying any attention to research in the field.

## How Can Organizations Go from Where They Are to Where They Need to Be?

For some organizations, things will have to get worse before they get better. For other, more enlightened organizations, the major change is likely one of leadership, both within the L&D organization and in the organization itself. This also includes changes in HR, which often really messes up L&D when they get hold of it. I think the way we train and certify L&D professionals is not just weak, but it is so tied to traditional education theory and practice that we can't shake our paradigms. And the proliferation of technology is not helping, as too many organizations see technology as the solution. "Just give me an LMS and our training problems will be over!" We need a better understanding of strategy and more discipline. But most of all, we need real, understandable, and enlightening success stories and case studies. Sometimes, the consequences of our actions are not significant to make us change. Perhaps that is why the military has always been more innovative in L&D (of course, they have the money, too).

# SECTION 4

# PATH FORWARD

The path forward is to break our strategy into concrete steps and then consider how we will move forward in light of the pragmatics and likely future.

# 10

# Re-Do

To implement the shift in strategy, we need a very clear focus on performance in the moment and on development over time. For optimal execution, we want to address the barriers, needs, and opportunities. Ideally, we can curate resources and solutions rather than create. From there, if we determine that the solution is something that P&D needs to design, we will need effective learning or performance support design. For continual innovation, we need facilitation, focusing both on the individual and larger aggregations of work teams and communities.

The notion in redefining performance and development is to focus on two complementary areas. One area is *performance consulting*, which looks at optimizing execution in the moment by analyzing tasks and root causes and developing or sourcing appropriate solutions, in the context of a performance ecosystem. The other area is *development facilitation*, which is focused on continual improvement and innovation. Here the focus is more on helping people improve while working on their own and together. There is overlap, as some of the performance solutions will come from the network, and some of the facilitation will be to improve problem solving in the service of performance, so the roles are linked at the wrists and ankles, but the methods are different.

## PERFORMANCE CONSULTING

Our short-term goal is supporting the performance goals of the organization. Given the increasing complexity with which we must deal, efficiency of operations runs a close second to impact on the organization. We must avoid developing anything we do not have to. On the execution side, our role has to be as performance consultants (Robinson & Robinson, 2008).

To focus on performance, we need to identify the performance metrics we need to meet. Is it external, like customer satisfaction or sales? Is it internal, like time to troubleshoot, rate of new product generation, or time to market? We should also be able to impact time to productivity, retention, and employee satisfaction. We may also be shooting for goals like ability to conduct useful searches, navigate the organizational systems, and interact with others in productive and constructive ways (which may have direct impacts as well).

From the business need, we can evaluate what the appropriate support solution needs to be. Our analysis process will have to take into account the different opportunities and provide maps to solutions. We have to take advantage of all the resources that can impact performance. We must leverage the network and communities and performance support, as well as formal learning. And we may be shifting the relative priorities.

To succeed, we need a new perspective. In computer science, there's a concept called "lazy evaluation," where a statement that can avoid being processed should be. For instance, if you have a statement *X or Y*, and you already have evaluated X and find it to be true, you don't need to evaluate Y, since either is sufficient. In our case, this means we shouldn't develop a solution if a resource already exists. It can come from outside providers, through the network, or developed by communities internally. You will want to evaluate the cost versus developing your own, but your accounting should include lost opportunities to work on other topics.

Overall, both a broader analysis process and a more flexible design process are needed to deliver solutions.

### Broader Analysis

How does our analysis process change? The human performance technology (HPT) approach (Pershing, 2006) is a good start, in that it goes beyond courses to identify not just the performance gap, but the root cause of the gap, and to align solutions to that cause. Our analysis has to identify whether the gap between desired performance and existing performance is due to a skill gap, a lack of information, a lack of motivation, or another cause. We must avoid determining that a course is the answer until we identify a significant skill gap (or knowledge that *must* be in the head and is as yet not there), as opposed to other problems.

Our approach has to be laser-focused on metrics that we are trying to impact. We have to partner with the executives about what needles need to be moved, and then use our best tools to address those gaps. We can't just take business executives' intuition about what's needed or orders for what they want, but instead we have to take ownership of what the answer to the measurable need is. This is not to say that this will be easy, as it is an organizational change, but it is one that, ultimately, will lead to better organizational outcomes.

One caveat is that our experts cannot actually tell us what they do (Clark & Estes, 1996). When we are trying to unpack the elements of successful performance, we need to go deeper than just ask experts. If we determine that there is a performance gap, we have to carefully evaluate whether, indeed, a skill gap exists or whether the problem lies elsewhere. This puts more responsibility on performance consultants than just trusting the subject matter expert (SME), but the benefit will be a much greater ability to impact performance. Dealing with SMEs can be challenging, but Aleckson and Ralston-Berg (2011) provide clues on how to establish credibility and leverage with SMEs in order to proceed productively.

Once we have done the initial needs analysis, which rightfully includes the context of performance, audience, and more, our focus must shift to design.

## Backwards Design

With a focus on performance, we should look for solutions that will map to the cause and to our goals. The question is whether we need to optimize execution or whether our goal is to foster innovation. Is this a situation when we know what the answer should be, or will that solution need to be discovered? Should it be done alone or in conjunction with others? The solutions include performance support and the network, among others, in addition to courses.

We need to take the metrics we are attempting to impact and make a statement about how far we expect to be able to move them with our interventions, and then set that as our target. We also should be setting a threshold below which there is insufficient impact. The point is to find ways to evaluate our impact. We should be testing our interventions to determine whether they are working or not, and we need criteria to make this determination.

At this stage, I argue we need to work backwards (see Figure 10.1). We need to identify the performance we desire and then decide how to distribute information among the individual, the network, and resources—digital and real. The strong implication is that, as much as possible, we should resist trying to change the individual, as this is difficult. There are certainly times it is necessary, but drawing on our understandings of cognition, we should recognize that developing skills is a challenging prospect, and developing rote information is even more challenging.

Our focus must be on how we want people to perform, and we must figure out what can be "in the world" (up to and

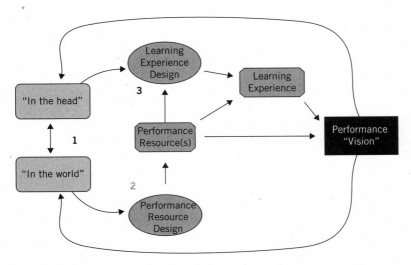

**Figure 10.1**   Backwards Design

including "everything"), and then what has to be "in the head." From there, we can design the resources (or make them available, in the case of networks) and, only then, design any needed learning experiences.

The principle here is to recognize that, when we want people to perform in a resourced environment, we should develop the formal learning to incorporate the performance resources in the experience. If we can avoid formal learning, we can and should, but when we can't, we should develop the resources before we develop the training.

The resources we have "to hand" need to be broad. We [should] have the network, we have performance support, and we have courses. Which do we use when? We must systematically determine the root cause of the problem and map that to the intervention. Is the problem a lack of sufficient resources, lack of knowledge or skills, or do we have a motivation problem? Wallace (2007) breaks down the potential causes as environmental problems, knowledge or skill problems, or individual factors. For our purpose here we are focusing largely on knowledge or skill problems, but our solutions are still richer than before.

If the issue is knowledge, we should absolutely determine whether it has to be in the learner's head or it can be in the world, either in a resource or the network (see Figure 10.2). If—as has been said—the value of employees is truly no longer what is in their heads but also what is in their networks, we should not develop resources we do not need to develop. And, again, we know that it is hard to get information into our heads.

Ideally, the information is in the world either from available resources or from the network. Secondly, we may have to

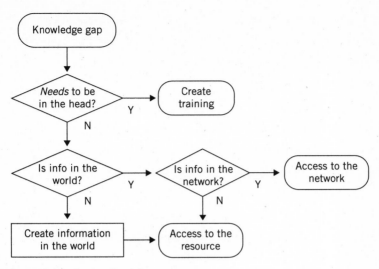

**Figure 10.2**  Design Decisions

design resources, even ones that leverage what is in individuals' heads. Worst case, we will have to put information in the head (for instance, if it needs to be there immediately).

Sometimes, it makes sense to look for information in the world. While the pragmatic reason for not having to develop resources is one opportunity, there are times when, on principle, one should look to the network for the answer, whether it exists or has to be created:

- When information is changing too fast to capture
- When the situation is too unique to be worth allocating resources
- When the situation is too new to have an existing answer
- When the need is such that interpersonal interaction is desirable

Skills are different. When the need is an ability to make decisions better or in new ways, it is time for a course. When we do create a course, we must pay attention to the best design possible.

We may also be training on how things work and are accomplished in the organization, such as how resources are accessed and the local tools for communication and collaboration, in addition to proprietary processes. Processes outside organization-specific ones, however, are likely to be better explained through a good book or video on the topic, rather than through a course, or through courses others have developed.

## Specific Solutions

When solutions are designed, they have to follow certain principles, even if the solutions are very different from one another. The design for "in the head" is very different than design for "in the world," and both have levels of depth that are often ignored. If they are to be done, they should be done right.

Solutions in the head need to align with how we really learn. The changes in our understanding have helped identify why many of our existing "event-based" approaches don't work. As a consequence, we need new guidance. Julie Dirksen's *Design for How People Learn* (2012) is a lively, thoughtful, and thorough exploration of the fundamental principles that should be followed. Based on the latest research on learning, Dirksen's book lays out a systematic approach to meeting learning needs.

At core, one must start with meaningful outcomes and vetted business needs that, if effective, will address key performance indicators. These needs must focus on objectives for performance that are specific and measurable. Once the needs are identified, activities must be created that closely correspond to the problems in the work environment. Focusing on decisions that learners need to be able to make in the workplace is an effective way to both work with SMEs and to drive engaging challenges. A problem-centered approach has been shown to be effective, embedding the important decisions in a motivating context. Group work and discussion are often effective for learning, and they are engaging. Once learners are motivated to learn by using meaningful tasks, learning assets can be made available that support addressing the problems. Examples, both positive and negative, of the decisions they have to make facilitate an understanding of the underlying concept. This understanding supports transfer to appropriate (and no inappropriate) settings. How about great wins (and losses) in company lore? Using and communicating the rich conceptual models that should drive the decisions (and making them explicit in the examples) provides a sound basis for action in new situations.

The emotional side of the learning experience should not be neglected. Introductions to the experience should not only activate relevant prior knowledge but motivate the learners to embrace the coming experience. Examples should be chosen that apply the concepts to the work context in ways learners will recognize, ideally using story formats. Practice should also be meaningful in the context. The settings for the practice should mimic the emotional investment learners will have when really performing the task. An exaggeration of the context and consequences, or even fantastic settings, can make sense when far transfer is desired. Don't just have them make a sale, but make the sale that saves the company! Have them make a marketing campaign that overthrows an oppressive government, not just one that sells more widgets! I have argued that learning can, and should, be hard fun (Quinn, 2005), and it should be our mission when it comes to creating formal learning.

The nature of the learning experience also can, and should, change. The notion of a fixed learning path no longer makes sense. Computers can make a learning experience individualized, adapting to a learner's personal ability and interests. With the "Experience API," a richer suite of activities can support development of skills. Interviewing individuals, creating resources, solving problems, and capturing performance are all valid components for developing capability. Learning designs should represent a path to competency. While we may yet lack a learning design that is equipped to leverage real-world opportunities and serendipity, we should accept that learning is more than just an event.

Conrad Gottfredson and Bob Mosher's *Innovative Performance Support* (2011) provides an accessible overview of performance support and step-by-step approaches to develop the resources. The authors give guidelines not only for analysis and information design, but also for layout and delivery. Information architecture challenges, to make sure that resources are not only developed but also findable, are also covered.

Performance support resources should be matched to need. Visuals and narration (whether text-annotated images or verbally narrated video) can demonstrate procedures well. Decision trees might graphically portray the flow or interactively work with the performer in a mixed initiative dialog. Using both the right media for the message and appropriate design within the media is important. Text and graphic design for documents, audio production for audio support, and video production for visuals are all important.

Note that such rigor may not be necessary for user-generated resources. While it should not be assumed that users have design skills (and developing them may be a useful investment), the users' solutions can be shared and rated, worthy items rising to the top. Facilitators should review user-generated performance support for opportunities to benefit the organization as a whole. If the potential impact is significant and there are flaws that would prevent a resource from being fully utilized, there may be an opportunity for the facilitator to assist in a redesign.

The approach should always be iterative. Michael Allen, a leader in learning design approaches and development tools for decades, recently offered a development process that addresses the weaknesses of traditional approaches. Allen says that interface design has often provided insights for learning design and that components that manifest too infrequently in L&D approaches are iterative development with formative evaluation. He recommends leaving ADDIE for SAM (2012) and introduces the Successive Approximation Method, a very pragmatic framework for development that naturally incorporates iteration with staged development.

The underlying principle is to prototype with the lowest technology possible to gather feedback and then iterate. Have concrete goals for your intervention, and iterate until you achieve them. Gradually ramp up the fidelity of your prototype as you get closer, but lower investments up-front yield greater willingness to change. Higher use of tools early on increases the likelihood of resistance to fixing problems that emerge because of the investment. Our cognitive architecture causes us to fall into several design traps, including *functional fixedness*, where we don't see new uses of a tool, even though they are possible, and *set effects*, where we solve new problems with the same approach we used for previous problems, even though a new solution may be better.

Our design processes should tap into the same factors that we advocate for others: leverage diversity on the team, openness to new ideas, deliberate exploration of alternatives, and fair turn-taking. Systematic creativity is not an oxymoron. Although some of the traditional brainstorming techniques are not effective, more enlightened approaches yield better outcomes. Individuals who have the opportunity to generate their own ideas before hearing those of others, for instance, get the greatest divergence. Preventing premature evaluation of ideas similarly supports exploration of all ideas on the table before convergence.

At core, we should be using evidence-based approaches for our interventions, both on the performance side and on the facilitation side.

## DEVELOPMENT FACILITATION

When we facilitate, we try to improve outcomes against business objectives. Those elements are typically not performance execution issues, although they do have an impact. For instance, if someone needs an answer, that person's skills in securing support may have to be developed. We should help individuals to develop their own skills. This process will be hard to measure as business impact, but we can measure both the difference in business metrics between those who do and those who do not receive such facilitation. Ultimately, we can mine the impact of improving capability across the organization.

Our goal should be to start with basic information skills: the ability to search effectively, to evaluate the results of a search, and to share discovered solutions. Harold Jarche (2013) has developed a useful personal knowledge management (PKM) scheme that provides a good scaffolding, with stages of Seek, Sense, and Share. *Seek* includes skills in searching, discovering who to track in different media, and even how to ask for help or information. *Sense* comes from culling information and determining the underlying meaning: curating, analyzing, synthesizing, and meaning-making. *Share* is identifying elements to pass on and sharing one's own ideas and thoughts.

These skills should not be assumed, but detailed and developed, perhaps even assessed. This may come from workshops or ongoing monitoring and facilitation. Help-on-demand would make sense as well. Being explicit about the value of building knowledge tools and sharing them is a component of successful facilitation as well.

More broadly, people's skills for working well together should not be assumed. The early problem with email, when messages would be much less polite than face-to-face communications, illustrated that not everyone has well-developed social media skills. The ability to offer help in useful ways, conduct challenging conversations, and work together are not always fully distributed, face-to-face or online. Again, being concrete about the skills and explicitly facilitating them builds a learning organization.

## Getting Informal

Jay Cross, with his revolutionary book *Informal Learning* (2007), helped illuminate the opportunities to be found in looking beyond the course. The power of networks maps to learning as well as, or better than, it does to endeavors. The facilitation Cross proposed included going beyond skill development to structural mechanisms that promote interpersonal interaction. For example, putting the coffee machine near the mail distribution center increased the likelihood of conversations and desirable outcomes.

As things move faster, particularly in a learning culture, the likelihood that an answer will emerge from the people engaged in the work exceeds the likelihood that L&D can identify and develop the answer. The *Intellectual Capital* that Thomas Stewart presciently asked organizations to capitalize on (1999) means developing and facilitating networks.

Tony Bingham and Marcia Conner's *The New Social Learning* argued for looking at the social side of the picture. The book helped launch awareness of the possibilities (2010). The authors examined a suite of social tools, including blogs, microblogs, collaborative documents, and more. They also addressed criticisms and provided recommendations.

"Social" has brought with it some baggage that hinders its adoption. Many years ago, I was doing some work for a company that had purchased an IT infrastructure package to digitize their business (what would now be called enterprise resource planning or ERP software). The company had, however, asked the vendor to turn off email because they were afraid people would waste time discussing social events and the like. Now these people had phones and water coolers, so there wasn't a lack of social channels. Can you imagine doing business without email now (despite what might be fervent wishes to the contrary)? The problem was not the email, but the company not trusting people.

Even today, we see organizations blocking people from using social networks at their desks. It's not a problem with access, but about whether you trust people or not. However, it is increasingly being recognized that what people bring to the office is no longer just what is in their heads, but who they can connect with in their networks. Realistically, you cannot stop it; people can just head outside to use their mobile devices to check what's happening.

Your organization likely already has social media policies in place, because there are restrictions on what employees can and cannot say to other people on the phone or at parties. The same restrictions on what can be said face-to-face hold true for other forms of social interaction. The only caveat is that digital media can be tracked, so deniability is reduced. The best social media policies are only slightly less terse and irreverent than "don't be an idiot."

Social both augments formal and supports informal learning. The real opportunity for continual innovation will come from interaction both real and virtual, so the tools for the virtual must be in place, as well as a supportive culture. The goal is to open up to networks, not shut them down. However, we should not take for granted employees' ability to successfully navigate and leverage the network.

Jane Bozarth's *Social Media for Trainers* (2010) has laid the groundwork for using social tools to support formal learning. This book provides a useful overview of the social tools and specific recommendations for ways in which these tools can be used in meaningful ways to augment the classroom.

The various social media available provide new ways to communicate that supplement what can be done in the classroom. Taking and sharing photos or videos that relate to the subject matter help learners personalize and put the material in context. Synchronous channels like microblogs provide an alternate for what normally is a serial conversation. Discussion forums can augment classroom discussion, and blogs allow learners to reflect on what has happened.

Jane Hart's *Social Learning Handbook* (2014) focuses on the use of social media to support informal learning. The author looks at social media from the point of view of supporting workplace learning, arguably the most important perspective. The level of detail provided, with deep coverage of tools, useful evaluation frameworks, and more, is very useful for moving organizations forward.

Social media allow generating, finding, sharing, and adding value to content. Any social activity, even in communities, is largely personal in nature. Since individuals view it as coming from their own initiative, they feel a sense of ownership. Consequently, Hart recommends that companies support bottom-up usage, as opposed to imposing social from the top down.

## Meta-Learning

As mentioned earlier, we can and should be facilitating learning skills in our organizations. Learning to learn may be the best investment you can make in an era in which change is ever-present. Leaving meta-learning to chance risks having the organization perform less than optimally. Evaluating learning skills, and developing them in our employees, provides an enormous opportunity.

Learning skills cannot be developed in isolation, but must be layered on across meaningful activities. This can be done either through designed activities for learning or embedded work activities. The former is easier to manage, the latter more meaningful. In facilitation, opportunities for the latter emerge, particularly if activities are tracked, for instance, through the xAPI.

The basic idea is to make the underlying processes behind the thinking clear and visible. A useful approach is "learning and working out loud" or using an explicit policy to "narrate your work." An explicit description and discussion of one's thought processes as well as the outcomes facilitates one's ability to reflect on and refine his or her thinking. This process should be used whether in the classroom, online, or in the real workplace.

The skills required of a facilitator include the PKM and the SCANS competencies. Developing employees on general skills supports human resource goals of a demonstrable investment in the workforce to support retention, in addition to creating a more capable workforce.

## PRIORITIZATION

What has been implicit in this discussion, but must be made explicit, is the overall process of determining when and how to invest resources. For performance, the "least assistance principle" suggests letting the world provide the solution if possible. If the need is not skill development and ephemeral, unique, or already solved from curated or user-created resources, the network is a better solution than trying to develop resources. Point to existing resources, rather than develop others, if possible. If the need is skill development, and if coaching and more mentoring can help learners get where they need to be, this should be the default. Letting people help each other develop is another way to build up valuable social capital and use more natural learning paths.

Resources should be expended only when necessary. Performance support should be employed only when such support can be justified by improvements in outcomes over an extended time. Although the flexible revision of such resources, supporting reuse over time, can amortize up-front costs, the time rate of change versus the cost of revision must be evaluated. Similarly, with courses and formal learning, when the skill shift is significant and the cost of the development justifies the investment, only then should a course be developed.

In the long term, of course, more and more of this can and should be devolved to communities of practice (CoP). The communities should take ownership of their associated competencies and resources. With collaborative tools, CoPs can take ownership and be responsible for documenting paths to capability, as well as co-develop resources to support performance. This is where the facilitation role overlaps with performance, although there should always be a role for formal support.

This is not just a matter of pragmatics for managing limited resources, although such an argument is viable. On principle, supporting the ability of people to self-help is necessary owing to the increasing rate of change, and it empowers individuals to develop their skills and manage outcomes.

This is not to say that the strategy is entirely driven on principle, as pragmatics may play a role as well. Any organizational initiative planned or underway can be an opportunity to leverage that initiative for P&D goals.

For example, an investment in a content infrastructure, typically for web marketing, can be leveraged for performance usage as well. Social media or knowledge management similarly provide opportunities to support development. Exercises in restructuring, competencies, or other organization development initiatives also could provide opportunities for effecting change. Even tough economic times might provide an opportunity to discuss changes that will make the organization more effective.

While principled advancement is the rule, being opportunistic can streamline efforts or minimize investment. If the organization is already investing in certain changes, arguing for a marginal additional investment that yields significant benefits is worth exploring. To make the case for benefits, however, means being able to discuss measurable business impact.

## MEASURED

Our work has to be measured both for its formative and its summative impact. We need to measure what we do and how well we're doing it. We need to measure ourselves by our contributions to the organization and its endeavors. Benchmarking ourselves on efficiency makes sense after we have impact, but not before.

One of the surprising outcomes of Kirkpatrick's four levels of evaluation (Kirkpatrick & Kirkpatrick, 2005) is how it has been misused in organizations. The model stipulates:

1. *Subjective evaluation:* Do users think it's valuable?

2. *Performance change:* Can users perform the necessary new behavior?

3. *Workplace change:* Are users working differently?

4. *Workplace impact:* Is the user performance impacting business measures?

Kirkpatrick was very clear that you should start with Level 4 and work backward. Perhaps, then, he should have numbered in reverse order; the evidence is that most organizations start with Level 1, some measure Level 2, and the number evaluating Levels 3 and 4 drops off significantly (ASTD, 1996). Moreover, the implementation at several levels tends to fall short. Too often, the questions asked at Level 1 evaluate whether the users enjoyed the experience or the instructor and those asked at Level 2 evaluate whether the users have knowledge about what to do, rather than assessing their actual ability!

We should not be measuring a delta on a pre-test and post-test. One problem with this is that it begs the question of whether the post-test ability actually impacts the business. Worse, the post-test evaluates the ability of the learner to now perform the indicated skill, so a pre-test isn't necessary. We shouldn't have developed the learning experience if we didn't already know there was a need, and we should only be assessing ultimate success on the needed competency. I also have argued (Quinn, 2008) that pre-tests are user-abusive, as taking tests on things that should not be known yet is an undesirable experience. While evidence exists that it is helpful to have such pre-tests, that data has been generated for knowledge, not skill performance, and I suggest that the benefit comes from preparing the learner and that other methods are less onerous.

We should be factoring these impact goals into our formative evaluation as well. We should have metrics that we expect our interventions to achieve, whether on the performance or facilitation side, and we should be working to achieve those metrics. For both formal learning and performance support, we should have usability goals to complement our evaluation of impact, because if we are not achieving our goals, the question is whether the problem is bad design of the intervention or bad interface design. Typically, usability is measured by time to accomplish the goal, errors in performance, learnability, relearnability, and preference. For formal learning, we should also evaluate engagement via a subjective evaluation.

And we should be iterating until we achieve our goals. If we're not achieving them as fast as our resources are being expended, we can and should revisit our goals, but assuming that our efforts are valuable is an error of hubris. We should set targets to achieve and performance levels by which we revisit the overall project with a view to terminate (Figure 10.3). We should not assume we will get it right the first time, and we must be prepared to evaluate and refine (and build this into our timeline and budget expectations).

Our testing should also move closer and closer to the real audience. In general, we should test first on ourselves, then on others who are convenient, and gradually work up to tests with real users, but this is not always feasible. Piloting should be done strategically. In general, experiments with a high expectation of failure are a reason to keep innovating, both at the organizational level and within P&D.

The capability provided by new standards for reporting, whether Experience API or what is emerging from the IMS Global Learning Consortium (Brandon, 2013), gives us rich tools for tracking results. With data generated through

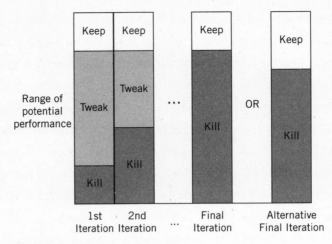

**Figure 10.3** Iterative Measurement

assessment tools and the ability to tap into and link data across systems, coupled with powerful analytics, any barrier to meaningful measurement is no longer about ability, but about the will to do it.

## TECH

The technology we have already is formidable. Tools exist that make creating even deeply immersive experiences within the grasp of the talented and resourced designer. We can decouple our support from the desktop as well and reach individuals whenever they need it wherever they are. We can facilitate important conversations and collaboration at any time or over time, overthrowing the tyranny of time and distance. We effectively have magic at our disposal, limited not by technology, but only by our imaginations.

We have the ability to create contextualized practice, from simple simulated interpersonal interactions to social 3D experiences. We can create compelling situations in which to practice decisions and skills, engaging learners' hearts as well as their minds. And we should! Whether the experience comes from a serious desktop game, virtual world, or mobile-enabled alternate reality game, we have the capability and should apply it when learning is the answer. Our resources might preclude using the highest technology solution, but if we get the cognitive and emotional challenge right, a number of viable options are available, and we can evaluate the tradeoffs between fidelity versus cost in terms of audience and expected impact.

Similarly, we are enabled through new technologies that push our performance support in new directions. Contextual relevance can be brought to wherever we are. The capabilities already deliverable by smart phones with cameras and compasses allow layering information around the world. The new digitally enabled glasses and watches enable new forms of interaction, and one of the prime areas of functionality can be learning. Content and interaction can be available both to augment existing contexts and to create new contexts for learning.

## Social

Another category of tool that works across niches is social. Social media can augment formal learning, support performance, and provide a mechanism for the communication and collaboration that drives innovation as well as facilitation. Different tools within the social provide capabilities that allow their inherent capabilities to be leveraged. The way to avoid hype is to truly understand what the opportunities are.

Our initial tools, beyond correspondence, were phones and email, with phones supporting synchronous verbal communication and email for asynchronous text. Chat and text messages provide a tool for synchronous communication (and, arguably, voicemail is an asynchronous tool). We also developed the capability for network-supported voice and video as well. Each of these has been "point to (multi)point" communication in that a specific recipient or group was targeted, as opposed to broadcast mass media that was available to anyone who tuned in.

A new model emerged from the network, more akin to mass media, where anyone could broadcast text (via a blog), audio (via podcasts), or video (via vidcasts). Sites also emerged that supported multiple media, so you could host a profile and share text, images, videos, or more, whether your own or pointing to others. Other individuals could subscribe to a feed or a particular channel, creating custom information sources. Individuals became curators of information. Distinctions emerged with sites and tools that specifically focused on different types of communication, specifically, microblogs for sharing limited text and images.

A new category of collaborative documents has emerged that allow more than one individual to collaborate on a document. Originally text, now such capabilities have spread to standard spreadsheets, presentations, and even diagrams. While currently somewhat limited compared to industrial-strength tools, the ability to continually edit instead of mailing files from one person to another has led to considerable benefits to organizations.

An important point is that different tools support different types of needs. Microblogs, for instance, are not deep reflection tools, with limitations on the quantity of information. However, because of the terse content, microblogs serve as quick pointers and question-asking that can reach an audience when you don't know who might have access to the answer. Blogs, on the other hand, serve for deeper reflection and support more engaged comments, but might be perused by a more limited audience. Collaborative documents allow people to produce tangible products with richer input and quicker time to finish.

We often neglect well-established technologies, so tools like email discussion forums are considered outdated. Similarly, chat compares unfavorably to microblogs, yet each has a unique capability. Rather than chasing trends, we should establish the key capabilities of each technology and use the right tool for the job.

P&D should understand not only learning and performance, but also communication and collaboration, as well as or better than anyone else does. Consequently, P&D should take the responsibility for facilitating the optimal use of these tools for the organization's benefit. IT may be responsible for maintaining the tools, perhaps even choosing them (to meet their goals of maintaining reliability and security, ideally, with P&D input), and other business units may have vested interests, but P&D should seize the opportunity before another group does, as the potential business benefits are too powerful to ignore.

P&D also has the imperative to experiment with tools for facilitating learning, performance support, and social interaction. The mantra of a culture of experimentation holds true, not only for the organization as a whole, but for P&D specifically. It is necessary both for learning and for facilitating.

### Infrastructure

Mobile technologies are bringing desktop capabilities to wherever we are. As a platform, mobile devices enable many of the same things, with a unique twist. Instead of smart phones being used for course delivery, they can serve to augment formal learning. For performance support, they can deliver not just standard (albeit streamlined) job aids, but can do so contextually. Social interaction can be decoupled from the desktop, and can leverage contextual information as well.

Across platforms, desktop and mobile, we must integrate the underlying technologies into accessible frameworks. A simple approach is to layer another level of portal on top of the existing hierarchy, integrating them into a user-centric framework supporting all potential categorization schemes and adding a robust search engine. The extra work can be traded off against the more seamless and streamlined user experience and more effective performance.

A second level of resource capability that would be useful is to go beyond static job aids to interactive decision support. The model is a performance wizard that can interact with users to scaffold information gathering. With such a mixed-initiative dialog, a system can support performers in executing important tasks.

A further opportunity is the need to be more systematic and structured about content development at the back end. As Chad Udell aptly points out in *Learning Everywhere* (2012), organizations need a content strategy. They require governance to oversee the content lifecycle and "content engineering" to develop appropriate tagging schemes and templates that support content by description instead of by hard-linking. Reuben Tozman details the components and opportunities in *Learning on Demand* (2012) and helps us recognize that the capability is imminent.

The goal is a rich infrastructure tying together the underlying systems to deliver rule-based performance experiences (see Figure 10.4). A partnership with IT is a necessary

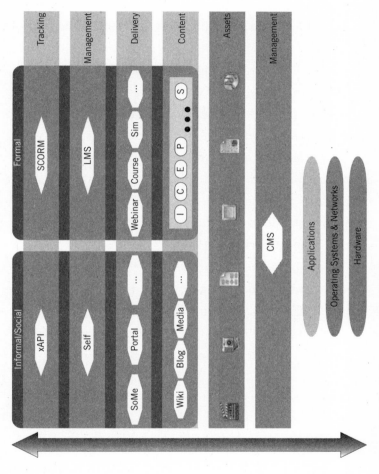

**Figure 10.4** Performance Infrastructure

component. Functional requirements must be defined so that underlying systems can be created.

The framework should support both formal and informal learning, incorporating media assets from a content management system running on an IT infrastructure (whether cloud or local). Those assets, whether P&D or user-generated or curated, can be delivered on request. The goal is to tie the entire system into a user-centric environment for performance.

We can—and should—apply the new tools of analytics to data generated across this infrastructure and look for emergent patterns. We need to "instrument" our tools—social network, learning environment, performance support tools, etc.—with data tracking such as the xAPI. We should look at this data to detect patterns and start sharing outcomes. The combination of intended evaluations and emergent patterns gives us a richer framework to move forward.

The penultimate goal is a performance ecosystem where the tools are to hand for individuals, teams, and communities within (and without) the organization to perform and innovate. The ultimate goal is for that environment to be intelligently adapted to the ongoing needs of stakeholders and the organization.

## PRAGMATICS

As suggested, many elements go along with this new focus. Design processes will change, content development processes will change, and there will be new requirements for data gathering, evaluation, and governance. All told, we need to take a strategic approach (see Figure 10.5).

Our strategy has to align a number of elements. Our vision has to guide a strategic plan that integrates a series of tactics

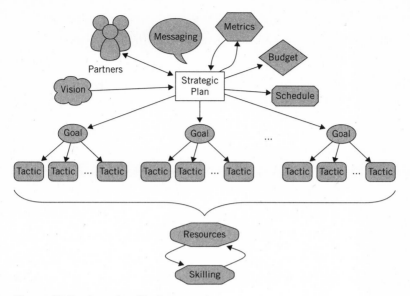

**Figure 10.5** Learning Strategy

to achieve the desired goals. We must work with our fundamental and strategic partners for governance and alignment. We must know metrics for what we're trying to achieve and metrics that tell us how we are doing. We'll need a schedule and a budget to manage our strategy. We should message our intentions, successes, and appreciation. And we must evaluate our resources and continually learn new skills to be able to execute our tactics.

Our vision has to be at a higher level than just developing any requested courses. We have to offer real business value by impacting the overall execution and innovation of the organization. This will come from being clear about the metrics we are trying to impact.

We have to look at the necessary partnerships. IT will be a fundamental partner, as will any specific business unit being served. Strategic partners will be those who can either facilitate or hinder our success. Potential partners include finance, legal, HR, and other executive functions. They need to be kept informed, as well as incorporated into the governance function. The role for P&D here is to provide strategic oversight and support.

Governance will need separate metrics to execute the oversight role. While the guiding committee examines impact outcomes for effectiveness, the strategic oversight role also requires examining efficiencies.

We must account for and then prioritize our budget and schedule. The largest part of the strategy for a shift to this new focus will be assessing the current state and choosing the path to take to where we intend to be. This situation will vary by organization, given the existing state, strengths, focuses, and nature of that organization. Retail, for example, would likely benefit from a different sequence of transformations than an engineering organization would.

Our messaging has to be strategic as well. This strategy is an organizational change, and it needs to be treated as such. While written specific to elearning, Jay Cross and Lance Dublin's *Implementing e-Learning* (2002) covers a lot of the mapping of organizational change to the learning function and serves as a useful guide to what we have discussed here. The overarching point is to communicate a vision, detail the benefits, assist the transformation, and reward behavior in line with the changes.

Our goals and tactics must cover the processes we want to execute. To transition from where we are now to where we want to be, we must understand what our processes need to be and then figure out a sensible sequence of steps to arrive at our destination. Our support processes must see opportunities to optimize execution and facilitate innovation. We need to scan for needs and partner with other units to identify opportunities, as well as monitor communities and work teams. And we want our steps to build upon one another, so that later work can leverage what has already been accomplished.

When we identify an opportunity to create support and/or a learning experience, our design processes should start with measurable deficits that can be addressed. We then align our outcomes to impact real business metrics.

Our facilitation processes also, ideally, have metrics, whether direct impact on the business or meaningful activity that can be inferred to be a contribution. Our goal should be both optimizing the interactions that lead to innovation as well as optimizing execution of the known processes.

We have to self-assess our own skills and develop any necessary new skills. The LPI Capability Map (see Appendix A) or the ASTD Competency Model (see Appendix C) provide useful evaluation mechanisms and guidance for moving forward.

## BOTTOM LINE

We have a vision of what a redo looks like:

- An overall focus on facilitating organizational success.
- One component is optimizing execution.
- The other component is facilitating innovation.

*(Continued)*

- We must align design processes with our understanding.

- We need to measure what we do.

- We must leverage technology affordances in alignment with our goals.

- We need to be strategic in our implementation.

With these elements in hand, we are equipped to move forward.

# 11

# Moving Forward

The question is: What are you going to do differently today and tomorrow on the way to next month and next year? The short answer is change. Unless you're already performance-focused, optimizing execution, and facilitating innovation, there's room for improvement.

The very first thing to do is to stop doing what we are doing. That, arguably, is impossible, yet there needs to be fundamental change. We have to stop being order-takers and start being performance consultants and improvement facilitators. We need to stop taking what SMEs say they do and what people need, and really investigate. And we have to stop believing we can get meaningful behavior change out of an information dump.

We have to stop doing what we are doing in a vacuum. We need to be partners with the organizational units in the organization, whether sales teams, faculty members, engineering groups, managers, or executives. We need to find out what metrics they care about, what data they use to evaluate how they are doing, and then be partners in moving those measures in positive ways. And we need to monitor what is happening in related fields.

It's going to be difficult to convince the top of the organization that it is important to shift resources. Yet, the alternative is a slow path to extinction. Increasingly, businesses can find alternatives to the services of L&D, such as user-generated video portals, social networking tools, and rapid elearning tools. L&D has to shift to making a measurable contribution to the organization.

We must rethink the role of L&D. It's about performance, directly and via development. It's about using all available tools. It's about empowering people via a learning culture and giving ongoing support at every level. It's about impacting the organization in measurable and important ways.

This will take a mental mind shift: P&D must be willing to release control. P&D cannot make people learn; enabling learning has been and always will be problematic. It's important to find all the ways we can to assist people in performing as they need to, including helping them to help themselves.

## PARALLEL PATHS

Several of our activities can and should be accomplished in parallel. Each area of endeavor—culture, strategy, formal learning, performance support, social, infrastructure—will require its own initial steps. The appropriate steps and sequence will, of course, depend on where the organization and the P&D department currently are.

The path to an empowering culture is challenging, and this is out of the control of the P&D group. Culture change is hard, even when everyone is committed to it. P&D has to evangelize the message in the organization as a whole while practicing what is preached within P&D.

For formal interventions, the goal is to shift to performance consulting and to integrate performance support and courses (whether training or general education in nature) into a unified approach. Start with addressing real needs and identifying root causes. From there, determine the appropriate balance between courses and job aids. Whatever is done should be done well. Courses should meet evidence-based standards for good learning design. Courses that result in knowledge dump and test when a skill shift is needed or when a job aid is sufficient must be eliminated. We must align our efforts with what is known about facilitating learning and performance.

On the social side, in addition to modeling and developing a sharing culture, we have to provide the infrastructure for and promote and develop communities. Look for existing communities to leverage, and help them reach a self-sustaining level of capability. You also want the social infrastructure to support work teams. You want tools that support a variety of communication needs, from reflective discussion to quick answers, and collaboration needs across formats. To move forward, start developing the infrastructure and putting it to work for the early adopters, sharing the best practices that emerge and facilitating the outcomes as uptake spreads.

We also must refine the information architecture around performance. Our information resources and social support need to reflect the users' perspective, not the perspective of various business units. We need to be community-, task-, and performer-focused when supplying resources to meet users' needs, applying good information architecture. We also must build up our content processes to facilitate more intelligent content delivery and manage the content lifecycle. Reengineering the content processes should center around formal delivery so that, ultimately, user-generated content will both be accessible and supported through a lifecycle.

New skills are required. Rather than sourcing those skills by hiring new staff, we should look within. Many of the core skills are likely to be available or able to be developed within the existing team. Our investment in the team can herald a shift to a new learning culture, and the team can help and support this shift. An obvious first step is for the P&D leader to start sharing and experimenting, expecting the team members to do the same. The leader should also develop a skills-mapping exercise and lead discussion about who moves where and when.

Strategically, the P&D leader has to lay out the steps that are required while sending messages to the rest of the organization about the intended changes.

Different businesses have different priorities. Firms that typically employ a rotating cast of young folks will be more interested in improving execution rapidly. An advanced manufacturing firm will need to get more innovation from their experts, who are often insular. The focus must be on supporting existing tasks first, then moving the organization in the direction it needs to go.

Going forward, stakeholders in other business units will own the important metrics, and partnerships with others to augment the change will be necessary. Selling the change is key to convince executives, stakeholders, employees—potentially even the P&D team itself—of the need. Developing a business case is a good place to start, to convince yourself as much as anyone.

## THE MONEY STORY

When it comes to finding the money to make the change, the first argument is simple: the existing metrics used by L&D do not have a mechanism to support evaluating their impact on the business. Benchmarking efficiency is not the same as demonstrating the real value of money spent in terms of impact on the organization.

The initial argument is intuitive: expending effort on measurably improving the organization has to be a better use of resources. However, we must back up this argument with real measurements. This will be challenging unless we gain the support of the operations functions within the organization, such as IT and finance. Having a discussion with them is one of the first steps in starting the change process.

The process should not be more onerous than other efforts to determine impact have been. The costs could be considered overhead or amortized across other initiatives. However, a real business case should be made for each new initiative. Root cause analysis should yield cost figures that can be weighed against estimates of intended benefits.

Improvements can come in a number of ways. Time to accomplish tasks can be reduced, such as time per customer service transaction or time to develop a new product. Errors might be reduced, in terms manufacturing defects, customer orders, or problem-solving recommendations. Other outputs might be increased, such as closed sales, new product ideas, or repeat customers. Customer satisfaction might be the ultimate metric.

Lay the costs to deliver improvements against these hypothesized improvements. For each intervention, make a business case. The leader of a learning unit I know created a template for his team to make the business case for any intervention that one of them thought would be a good idea. This both supported qualification of ideas out in the organization and raised awareness of the business mindset among his group. The costs should be the same as those used in calculating efficiency, but balanced against impact.

## THE LONG GAME

The argument here is not just for the world we live in now. This approach sets the stage for changes that are coming. Changes in society and technology that are still to come will make a performance focus even more important.

Societally, we have gained awareness of the benefits of diversity, the relevance of empowerment, and the importance of meaningfulness. As discussed previously, benefit corporations signal a change in beliefs about organizational goals. The importance of meaningful work in fostering positive employee relations is becoming evident. Diversity is increasingly being seen as a source of strength, both in organizations and in work teams.

Organizations need to align with new societal developments. Today's organizations will be more successful if they incorporate important societal trends and goals, or at least not violate ethical and moral guidelines. They will benefit if they empower their workers and give them support. They will benefit if they incorporate ways to continually innovate and improve. They can promote methods like the balanced scorecard approach (Kaplan & Norton, 1996), which includes learning and growth as a significant component of business strategy. Remember that P&D has to document the real impact they have on the organization.

Technology is becoming more sophisticated as well. New technology such as wearable computing (new "smart" glasses and watches) will increase our reach and capability. Coupled with ubiquitous networks and intelligently adaptive software, we in P&D will be able to customize support, achieving the "right stuff" prophesied by Wayne Hodgins (2002), paraphrased here: the right interaction at the right time and the right place to the right person in the right way on the right device.

I believe we still do not have a design approach that reaches where we can, and should, be going. We need, and will see, a new design that incorporates distribution across delivery channels, media, time, and more. The desired design process will support creating, at both a curricular and pedagogical level, rich activity-based learning experiences. Our learning solutions must stop being event-based and unitary experiences and start being continual and ubiquitous.

We have the opportunity to extend learning to create what I call Slow Learning, where the learning experience is paced at the rate at which our brains can accommodate it. Andrea Phillips, in her book *A Creator's Guide to Transmedia Storytelling* (2012), outlines how to design engaging experiences across contexts and time. We need a similar guide to transmedia learning and must learn how to create engaging learning experiences across contexts and time.

There also will be an architecture that supports not just a created learning experience, but an adaptive contextual learning experience. Ultimately, we will have devices with us that can serendipitously use contextual opportunities to develop our understanding. The system will draw upon the environment when possible and create contexts when necessary. Such a system could both support performance in the moment and develop people over time.

We should not stop there. When (not if) we achieve these ends, practicing what we preach requires that we share what we are learning and continue to develop our understanding together. We need continual innovation in our work teams, communities, and the larger network that connects us. I intend to post pointers to resources and communities at RevolutionizeLnD.com, where I hope you will join us.

Let me propose a stretch goal here. What we do, I suggest, is help people work smarter. Why not shoot for the next level: Can we help people work more wisely? While definitions differ, from a pragmatic perspective wisdom is increasingly under investigation. The goal is to make decisions that are right, not just for us and those near us, but for all, in both the short and long term, and this is teachable (Sternberg, 2001). The answers don't fully exist yet, but there are lots of hints.

Whether we take it the extra step, we can, and should, make a stand to contribute in measurable, significant, and strategic ways to the organization.

## CONCLUSION

Learning & Development is increasingly irrelevant in light of what we know and how things are changing. However, there is no need for a wholesale elimination of the unit, as a sound foundation exists for creating new ways. However, significant change is needed to get there.

The status quo has been resistant to change for a host of reasons. Lack of awareness, barriers to change, and vested interests are contributing factors. Regardless, we must push forward. Our organizations need it, our people need it, and society needs it. We have an important role to play, and we cannot abandon our responsibility.

The time for change is now. I hope you will join us by signing the Performance & Development Manifesto:

I, a Performance & Development innovator, hereby commit to the following principles:

1. Moving from a focus on learning to a focus on performance, integrating learning into work;

2. Building a culture of learning, communication, and collaboration;

3. Following the Least Assistance Principle;

4. Not taking orders, but determining business need and root cause;

5. Using all appropriate resources, not just training;

6. Avoiding resource development unless absolutely necessary: curation over creation;

7. Making use of the network a priority;

8. Choosing performance support over training when possible;

9. Doing it right when a course is needed: meaningful, minimal, with a maximum focus on practice and problem solving;

10. Building the infrastructure: content models, tagging and governance;

11. Explicitly facilitating learning and communication skills;

12. Addressing the full suite of solutions by working toward an integrated performance environment;

13. Evaluating what I do; and

14. Practicing what I preach: continual exploration and experimentation.

# References

Aleckson, J. D., & Ralston-Berg, P. (2011). *MindMeld: Micro-Collaboration Between eLearning Designers and Instructor Experts.* Madison, WI: Atwood Publishing.

Allen, M. (2012). *Leaving ADDIE for SAM: An Agile Model for Developing the Best Learning Experiences.* Alexandria, VA: ASTD Press.

American Society for Training & Development. (1996). *Restructuring: Results from the 1996 Benchmarking Forum.* Alexandria, VA: ASTD Press.

American Society for Training & Development. (2009). *Transforming Learning: Web 2.0 Technologies.* Alexandria, VA: ASTD Press.

American Society for Training & Development. (2010a). *Instructional Systems Design: Today and in the Future.* Alexandria, VA: ASTD Press

American Society for Training & Development. (2010b). *The Rise of Social Media: Enhancing Collaborations and Productivity Across Generations.* Alexandria, VA: ASTD Press.

American Society for Training & Development. (2011). *Better, Smarter, Faster: How Web 3.0 Will Transform Learning in High-Performing Organizations.* Alexandria, VA: ASTD Press

American Society for Training & Development. (2012a). *State of the Industry, 2012.* Alexandria, VA: ASTD Press

American Society for Training & Development (2012b). *Developing Results: Aligning Learning's Goals and Outcomes with Business Performance Measures.* Alexandria, VA: ASTD Press.

American Society for Training & Development. (2013). *Informal Learning: The Social Evolution*. Alexandria, VA: ASTD Press

Arneson, J., Rothwell, W.J., & Naughton, J. (2013). *ASTD Competency Study: The Training & Development Profession Redefined*. Alexandria, VA: ASTD Press.

Bassi, L., McGraw, K., & McMurrer, D. (2004). Using measurement to foster culture and sustainable growth. In M. Conner & J.G. Clawson (Eds.), *Creating a Learning Culture: Strategy, Technology, & Practice*. Cambridge, UK: Cambridge University Press.

Benedict, A., Esen, E., Williams, S., Handsman, R., Patton, D., & Rodeawald, P. (2008). *Critical Skills Needs and Resources for the Changing Workforce: Keeping Skills Competitive*. Alexandria, VA: Society for Human Resource Management.

Bingham, T., & Conner, M. (2010). *The New Social Learning: A Guide to Transforming Organizations Through Social Media*. Alexandria, VA: ASTD Press.

Blauth, C., McDaniel, J., Perrin, C., & Perrin, P.B. (2011). *Age-Based Stereotypes: Silent Killer of Collaboration and Productivity*. Tampa, FL: AchieveGlobal.

Bozarth, J. (2010). *Social Media for Trainers*. San Francisco, CA: Pfeiffer.

Brandon, B. (2013). IMS Global Learning Consortium: Interoperability Standards for Education. *Learning Solutions Magazine*. www.learningsolutionsmag.com/articles/1306/

Bransford, J.D., Brown, A.L., & Cocking, R.R. (Eds.). (2000). *How People Learn: Brain, Mind, Experience, and School*. Washington, DC: National Academy Press.

Bureau of Labor Statistics. (2013). Mass Layoffs–May 2013. USDL-13–1179

Business Week Online (1998). Steve Jobs on Apple's Resurgence: "Not a one-man show." *Business Week*. http://www.businessweek.com/bwdaily/dnflash/may1998/nf80512d.htm

Carroll, J.M. (1990). *The Nurnberg Funnel: Designing Minimalist Instruction for Practical Computer Skill*. Cambridge, MA: MIT Press.

Cattel, J. (2013). Housing a Love for Learning. *Chief Learning Officer, 12*(1), 22–25.

Chapnick, S. (2001). *The eLearning Readiness Assessment*. New York: Research Dog.

Clark, A. (1996). *Being There: Putting Brain, Body, and World Together Again*. Cambridge, MA: MIT Press

Clark, R.E., & Estes, F. (1996). Cognitive Task Analysis. *International Journal of Educational Research, 25*(5), 403–417.

Clark, R.C., & Mayer, R.E. (2003). *e-Learning and the Science of Instruction*. San Francisco, CA: Pfeiffer.

Clarke, A.C. (1984). *Profiles of the Future: An Inquiry into the Limits of the Possible* (rev. ed.). New York: Henry Holt & Co.

Clegg, E., & Quinn, C. N. (2004). The Agility Factor. In M. Conner & J.G. Clawson (Eds.), *Creating a Learning Culture: Strategy, Technology, and Practice*. Cambridge, MA: Cambridge University Press.

Coffield, F., Moseley, D., Hall, E. & Ecclestone, K. (2004). *Should we be using learning styles? What research has to say to practice.*London: Learning and Skills Research Centre.

Collins, A., Brown, J.S., & Holum, A. (1991). Cognitive Apprenticeship: Making Thinking Visible. *American Educator, 6*(11), 38–46.

The Community Roundtable. (2009). The Community Maturity Model. www.communityroundtable.com/research/community-maturity-model/

Cross, J. (2007). *Informal Learning: Rediscovering the Natural Pathways That Inspire Innovation and Performance*. San Francisco, CA: Pfeiffer.

Cross, J., & Dublin, L. (2002). *Implementing eLearning*. Alexandria, VA: ASTD Press.

Cross, J., & Quinn, C. (2002). The Value of Learning About Learning. Meta-Learning Lab. www.quinnovation.com/LearningAbout Learning.pdf

Davidson, C. (2012). *Now You See It: How Technology and Brain Science Will Transform Schools and Business for the 21st Century*. New York: Penguin.

de Jager, P. (2010). *A Pocketful of Change*. Brampton, Canada: de Jager & Company, Ltd.

Dirksen, J. (2012). *Design for How People Learn*. Berkeley, CA: New Riders Press.

Frey, T. (2006). Are You Acceleration Aware? *The Futurist*. http://futurist.typepad.com/my_weblog/2006/12/are_you_acceler.html

Garvin, D.A., Edmondson, A.C., & Gino, F. (2008, March). Is Yours a Learning Organization? *Harvard Business Review*, *86*(3), 109–116, 134.

Gawande, A. (2010). *The Checklist Manifesto: How to Get Things Right*. New York: Metropolitan Books.

Gery, G. (1991). *Electronic Performance Support Systems*. Available at Amazon.com.

Glushko, R. (2013). *The Discipline of Organizing*. Cambridge, MA: MIT Press.

Gottfredson, C., & Mosher, B. (2011). *Innovative Performance Support: Strategies and Practices for Learning in the Workflow*. New York: McGraw-Hill.

Gray, D. (2012). *The Connected Company*. Sebastopol, CA: O'Reilly Media.

Hart, J. (2014). *Social Learning Handbook*. Centre for Learning & Performance Technologies: c4lpt.co.uk.

Helsper, E., & Enyon, R. (2009). Digital Natives: Where Is the Evidence? *British Education Research Journal*, *36*(3).

Hodgins, W. (2002). Are We Asking the Right Questions? *Transforming Culture: An Executive Briefing on the Power of Learning*. Charlottesville, VA: University of Virginia, The Batten Institute at the Darden Graduate School of Business Administration.

Husband, J. (2013). What Is Wirearchy? http://wirearchy.com/what-is-wirearchy/

Hutchins, E. (1996). *Cognition in the Wild*. Cambridge, MA: MIT Press.

Jarche, H. (2013). Personal Knowledge Management. www.jarche.com/wp-content/uploads/2013/03/PKM-2013.pdf

Jennings, C. (2013). *70:20:10 Framework Explained*. Surrey Hills, UK: 70:20:10 Forum Pty Ltd.

Johnson, S. (2010). *Where Good Ideas Come From: The Natural History of Innovation*. New York: Penguin.

Kahneman, D. (2011). *Thinking, Fast and Slow*. New York: Farrar, Straus and Giroux.

Kaplan, R.S., & Norton, D.P. (1996). *The Balanced Scorecard: Translating Strategy into Action*. Boston, MA: Harvard Business School Press.

Katz, J. (2010). Beyond the Hype: Understanding HTML5 and its Potential for e-Learning and mLearning. *Learning Solutions*. www.learningsolutionsmag.com/articles/465/

Kelly, D. (2012). Is Content Curation in Your Skill Set? It Should Be. *Learning Solutions*. www.learningsolutionsmag.com /articles/1037/is-content-curation-in-your-skill-set-it-should-be

King, B. (2011). Too Much Content: A World of Exponential Information Growth. *Huffington Post*. www.huffingtonpost.com /brett-king/too-much-content-a-world-_b_809677.html

Kirkpatrick, D.L., & Kirkpatrick, J.D. (2005). *Transferring Learning to Behavior: Using the Four Levels to Improve Performance*. San Francisco, CA: Berrett-Koehler.

Koedinger, K.R., Corbett, A.C., & Perfetti, C. (2012). The Knowledge-Learning-Instruction (KLI) Framework: Bridging the Science-Practice Chasm to Enhance Robust Student Learning. *Cognitive Science, 36*(5), 757–798.

Landau, V., & Clegg, E. (2009). *The Engelbart Hypothesis: Dialogs with Douglas Engelbart*. Huntington, NY: NextPress.

Learning and Performance Institute. (2013, June). The LPI Capability Map: Six Month Report. Learning & Performance Institute Limited. www.learningandperformanceinstitute.com

Locke, C., Levine, R., Searles, D., & Weinberger, D. (1999). *The Cluetrain Manifesto*. New York: Perseus Books.

Manhertz, H., Jr. (2009). *The Generational Divide: Crucial Consideration or Trivial Hype?* Tampa, FL: AchieveGlobal.

Means, B., Toyama, Y., Murphy, R., Bakia, M., & Jones, K. (2009). *Evaluation of Evidence-Based Practices in Online Learning: A Meta-Analysis and Review of Online Learning Studies*. Washington, DC: U.S. Department of Education. www.ed.gov/about/offices/list /opepd/ppss/reports.html

O'Reilly, T. (2005). *What Is Web 2.0: Design Patterns and Business Models for the Next Generation of Software.* Sebastopol, CA: O'Reilly Media. http://oreilly.com/pub/a/web2/archive/what-is-web-20.html

Overton, L., & Dixon, G. (2013). The New Learning Agenda—Talent: Technology: Change. Towards Maturity. www.towardsmaturity.org/2013benchmark

Pagano, K.O. (2013). *Immersive Learning: Designing for Authentic Practice.* Alexandria, VA: ASTD Press.

Pashler, H., McDaniel, M., Rohrer, D., & Bjork, R. (2008). Learning Styles: Concepts and Evidence. *Psychological Science in the Public Interest, 9*(3), 105–119.

Pershing, J.A. (2006). *Handbook of Human Performance Technology: Principles, Practices, Potential.* San Francisco, CA: Pfeiffer.

Phillips, A. (2012). *A Creator's Guide to Transmedia Storytelling: How to Captivate and Engage Audiences Across Multiple Platforms.* New York: McGraw-Hill.

Pink, D. (2011). *Drive: The Surprising Truth About What Motivates Us.* New York: Riverhead Books.

Pontefract, D. (2013). *Flat Army: Creating a Connected and Engaged Organization.* San Francisco, CA: Jossey-Bass.

Quinn, C.N. (2005). *Engaging Learning: Designing e-Learning Simulation Games.* San Francisco, CA: Pfeiffer.

Quinn, C.N. (2008). The Case Against Pre-Testing for Online Courses. *eLearnMag.* http://elearnmag.acm.org/featured.cfm?aid=2139006

Quinn, C.N. (2009). Social Networking: Bridging Formal and Informal Learning. *Learning Solutions.* www.learningsolutionsmag.com/articles/57/social-networking-bridging-formal-and-informal-learning

Quinn, C.N. (2010). Better Design Doesn't Take Longer! *eLearnMag.* http://elearnmag.acm.org/featured.cfm?aid=1806335

Quinn, C.N. (2011). *Designing mLearning: Tapping Into the Mobile Revolution for Organizational Performance.* San Francisco, CA: Pfeiffer.

Quinn, C.N. (2012a). Content Systems: Next Generation Opportunities. www.learningsolutionsmag.com/articles/57/social-networking-bridging-formal-and-informal-learning

Quinn, C.N. (2012b). The Next Step for Learning: Practical Contextualization. *Learning Solutions*. www.learningsolutionsmag.com/articles/1028/the-next-step-for-learning-practical-contextualization

Quinn, C.N., Mehan, H., Levin, J.A., & Black, S.D. (1983). Real Education in Non-Real Time: The Use of Electronic Message Systems for Instruction. *Instructional Science, 11*, 313–327.

Robinson, D.G., & Robinson, J.C. (2008). *Performance Consulting: A Practical Guide for HR and Learning Professionals*. San Francisco, CA: Berrett-Koehler.

Rosenberg, M.J. (2006). *Beyond e-Learning: Approaches and Technologies to Enhance Organizational Knowledge, Learning, and Performance*. San Francisco, CA: Pfeiffer.

Rossett, A., & Shafer, L. (2006). *Job Aids and Performance Support: Moving from Knowledge in the Classroom to Knowledge Everywhere*. San Francisco, CA: Pfeiffer.

Sachs, J. (2012). *Winning the Story Wars: Why Those Who Tell (and Live) the Best Stories Will Rule the Future*. Boston, MA: Harvard Business School Press.

Sawyer, K. (2008). *Group Genius: The Creative Power of Collaboration*. New York: Basic Books.

Secretary's Commission on Achieving Necessary Skills. (1991). *What Work Requires of Schools: A SCANS Report for America 2000*. Washington, DC: United States Department of Labor. www.academicinnovations.com/report.html

Schwartz, N. (2010). Industries Find Surging Profits in Deeper Cuts. *New York Times*. www.nytimes.com/2010/07/26/business/economy/26earnings.html?pagewanted=all

Sternberg, R.J. (2001). Why Schools Should Teach for Wisdom: The Balance Theory of Wisdom in Educational Settings. *Educational Psychologist, 36*(4).

Stewart, T.A. (1999). *Intellectual Capital: The New Wealth of Organizations*. New York: Currency.

Strobel, J., & van Barneveld. A. (2009). When is PBL More Effective? A Meta-Synthesis of Meta-Analyses Comparing PBL to Conventional Classrooms. *Interdisciplinary Journal of Problem-Based Learning, 3*(1).

Taylor, D.H. (2013). Are You in the Training Ghetto? http://donaldhtaylor.wordpress.com/2013/04/15/are-you-in-the-training-ghetto/

Taylor, F.W. (1911). *The Principles of Scientific Management.* New York: Harper & Brothers.

Thalheimer, W. (2006a). *People Remember 10%, 20% . . . Oh Really?* Boston, MA: Work-Learning Research.

Thalheimer, W. (2006b). *Spacing Learning Events Over Time: What the Research Says.* Boston, MA: Work-Learning Research.

Torralba, F. (2008). Productivity Trends. *EconWeekly.* www.econweekly.com/2008/03/productivity-is-main-determinant-of.html

Tozman, R. (2012). *Learning on Demand: How the Evolution of the Web Is Shaping the Future of Learning.* Alexandria, VA: ASTD Press.

Udell, C. (2012). *Learning Everywhere: How Mobile Content Strategies Are Transforming Training.* Alexandria, VA: ASTD Press.

Vygotsky, L.S. (1978). *Mind in Society.* [M. Cole, V. John-Steiner, S. Scribner, & E. Souberman (Eds.)] Cambridge, MA: Harvard University Press.

Wallace, G. (2007). Lean-ISD. CADDI. http://eppicinc.files.wordpress.com/2010/07/lean-isd-book-pdf-2007.pdf

Wallace, G. (2011). 70 Percent of What an SME Knows Is Automated-Unconscious: Richard E Clark at USC CCT on SME Knowledge Being Automated and Unconscious. http://blip.tv/guy-w-wallace/70-percent-of-what-an-sme-knows-is-automated-unconsious-5099460

Warschauer, M. (2011). *Learning in the Cloud: How (and Why) to Transform Schools with Digital Media.* New York: Teachers College Press.

Wills, S., Leigh, E., & Ip, A. (2011). *The Power of Role-Based e-Learning.* New York: Routledge.

Wooley, A., & Malone, T. (2011). Defend Your Research: What Makes a Team Smarter? More Women. *Harvard Business Review.* http://hbr.org/2011/06/defend-your-research-what-makes-a-team-smarter-more-women/ar/

# Appendix A

# The LPI Capability Map

The Learning and Performance Institute, a global membership organization focused on the L&D community, has developed a map of capabilities for those engaged in this area. There's an associated self-assessment across levels of Practicing, Extending, Guiding, and Leading to be found at www.learningandperformanceinstitute.com.

| Category | Skill | Skill Definition |
|---|---|---|
| Live Delivery | Presentation delivery | *Presents to a live audience* |
| | Face-to-face delivery | *Live learning facilitation* |
| | Virtual/online delivery | *Virtual learning facilitation* |
| Learning Resources | Design | *Determining the design framework* |
| | Content creation | *Creating/using appropriate content* |
| Collaborative Learning | Supporting work teams | *Fostering collaboration* |
| | Supporting communities of practice (CoPs) | *Helping community managers to create and sustain CoPs* |
| | Supporting content co-creation and curation | *Helping groups create, curate, and share content* |
| | Developing collaborative learning skills | *Helping individuals develop collaborative learning skills* |
| Analysis and Strategy | Performance analysis | *Identifies performance gaps and defines appropriate solutions* |
| | Competency management | *Identifies and facilitates skills/knowledge competency* |
| | Assessment and evaluation | *Assessing and interpreting learning impact* |
| | Learning strategy | *Applying appropriate learning strategies* |

| | | |
|---|---|---|
| Learning Information Management and Interpretation | Information architecture | *Designing, implementing, and managing the virtual spaces that support and enable learning* |
| | Data interpretation | *Understanding and communicating data* |
| Learning Delivery Management | Project management | *Delivering projects* |
| | Change management | *Managing change* |
| Managing the Learning Function | People management and development | *Managing people* |
| | Process management and improvement | *Managing the learning function* |
| | Resource management | *Managing learning resources* |
| Business Skills and Intelligence | Financial management | *Controlling finances* |
| | Procurement | *Sourcing systems and services* |
| | Communication, marketing, and relationship management | *Promoting learning and performance* |
| | Industry awareness | *Monitoring industry developments* |
| Performance Improvement | Performance support | *Designs and provides resources to support workplace performance* |
| | Coaching | *Provides structured support and guidance to improve learner skills and performance* |
| | Mentoring | *Provides support and guidance to promote continuous professional development and career progression* |

# Appendix B

# The Towards Maturity Model

Towards Maturity is a benchmarking practice that provides authoritative research and expert consultancy services to help assess and improve the effectiveness and consistency of L&D performance within organizations. http://towardsmaturity.org/+

| Strand | Dimension | Description of Dimension and Example of Likert Statement from Survey |
|---|---|---|
| Defining Need | Alignment | There is a clear elearning strategy driven and measured by the business, e.g.: *There are measurable targets for learning and elearning.* |
| | Business need | Learning is aligned to work leading to relevant competencies/qualifications, e.g.: *Learning is relevant to current jobs.* |
| | Individual need | Learners gain competencies/qualifications relevant to their work and career, e.g.: *eLearning contributes to recognized qualifications.* |
| Learner Context | Choices | Learners have choices and personalized experiences, e.g.: *Staff have more control and visibility of their development.* |
| | Motivation | Learners are motivated, e.g.: *We support career aspirations (or personal job goals) with elearning.* |
| | Work-life balance | Learning is convenient and contributes to work/life balance, e.g.: *Managers give learners time to learn at home.* |
| Work Context | Managerial support | Managers provide support in the workplace, e.g.: *Managers coach their staff.* |
| | Technical environment | The technical environment supports learning anyplace, anytime, e.g.: *Our IT infrastructure will deliver learning to places convenient to staff.* |

| Building Capability | Learning & development (L&D) general skills | L&D specialists have appropriate approach, attitude, and contacts, e.g.: *Our internal training team members are willing to embrace new ways of working.* |
| | Assessment | L&D specialists are able to make best use of assessment tools, e.g.: *eLearning allows us to more closely simulate the work environment for assessment.* |
| | Facilitating collaboration | L&D specialists take advantage of informal learning, e.g.: *We encourage staff to help each other using discussion boards.* |
| | Learning design | L&D specialists are able to use a mixture of media and methods in learning design, e.g.: *eLearning in our organization is always part of a broad mix of methods.* |
| | Supporting learners | L&D specialists use a variety of electronic and personal methods to support e-learners at work, e.g.: *Learners have access to job aids.* |

*(Continued)*

| Strand | Dimension | Description of Dimension and Example of Likert Statement from Survey |
| --- | --- | --- |
| Ensuring Engagement | Empowering learners | Learners are equipped and informed to help them take advantage of available learning technologies, e.g.: *Staff know what learning is available for them.* |
| | Managers as stakeholders | Effective programs exist that engage managers as both users and key stakeholders, e.g.: *We equip line managers with resources and training so their teams get the most out of elearning.* |
| | Trainers as stakeholders | Effective programs exist that engage classroom trainers as both users and key stakeholders, e.g.: *Our face-to-face training courses integrate elearning content and support.* |
| | Change management | Change management and communications strategies are in place, e.g.: *We indentify and train local champions to act as change agents.* |
| Demonstrating Value | Feedback | Feedback is routinely collected from managers and learners, e.g.: *We routinely collect feedback from users of each course.* |
| | Measurement | Business measures and financial data are used in measurement of delivery and effectiveness, e.g.: *We measure specific business metrics when evaluating elearning effectiveness.* |
| | Communicating benefit | Business and staff success are regularly communicated to key stakeholders, e.g.: *We regularly communicate elearning successes to line managers and supervisors.* |

# Appendix C

# ASTD Competency Model

The American Society for Training and Development is the world's largest professional association dedicated to the training and development field. As part of their activities, they regularly review the necessary competencies required across the L&D area. The latest edition came out in 2013. You can find out more at www.astd.org.

| Area of Expertise | Description |
| --- | --- |
| Performance Improvement | Apply a systematic process for analyzing human performance gaps and for closing them. |
| Instructional Design | Design and develop informal and formal learning solutions using a variety of methods. |
| Training Delivery | Deliver informal and formal learning solutions in a manner that is both engaging and effective. |

*(Continued)*

| Area of Expertise | Description |
| --- | --- |
| Learning Technologies | Apply a variety of learning technologies to address specific learning needs. |
| Evaluating Learning Impact | Use learning metrics and analytics to measure the impact of learning solutions. |
| Managing Learning Programs | Provide leadership to execute the organization's people strategy; implement training projects and activities. |
| Integrated Talent Management | Build an organization's culture, capability, capacity, and engagement through people development strategies. |
| Coaching | Apply a systematic process to improve others' ability to set goals, take action, and maximize strengths. |
| Knowledge Management | Capture, distribute, and archive intellectual capital to encourage knowledge-sharing and collaboration. |
| Change Management | Apply a systematic process to shift individuals, teams, and organizations from current state to desired state. |
| Foundational Competencies | Knowledge, skills, abilities, and behaviors that are required for job success in most professional occupations, covering: business skills, global mindset, industry knowledge, interpersonal skills, personal skills, and technology literacy. |

# Index

Page references followed by *fig* indicate an illustrated figure; followed by *t* indicate a table.

# About the American Society for Training & Development

The American Society for Training & Development (ASTD) is the world's largest professional association dedicated to the training and development field. In more than 100 countries, ASTD's members work in organizations of all sizes, in the private and public sectors, as independent consultants, and as suppliers. Members connect locally in 130 U.S. chapters and with 30 international partners.

ASTD started in 1943 and in recent years has widened the profession's focus to align learning and performance to organizational results and is a sought-after voice on critical public policy issues. For more information, visit www.astd.org.